Preface

The stories in this book deal almost entirely with present-day life in the United States. They should be of particular interest to students who, while studying English, also want to learn something of the North American scene.

The stories fall within the form known as the short-short story. Stories of this type provide a convenient study medium, as each is only four or five pages long and can be studied easily within one or two class sessions.

Comprehension questions follow each story. These ten questions, and any others which a teacher may supplement them with, immediately test whether the students have a basic understanding of the story. Teachers should pay close attention to vocabulary, since not all students will understand all the terms used. The exercises should be written and may be supplemented at the teacher's discretion. Generally, the exercises use terms and structures from the story, so teachers have an additional opportunity to check understanding of vocabulary and grammar.

The discussion questions are new in this edition. Teachers

may use them to stimulate the students to use the vocabulary and structures from the story conversationally or for written work. A question such as "Why didn't Mr. Whitney call the police?" can be supplemented with "What did Mr. Whitney do instead of calling the police?" or "What would you have done in Mr. Whitney's situation?" Each question can thus lead to other questions and to interesting and lively class discussions.

Modern Short Stories in English is one of a series of three readers for students of English as a second language. The first, *Elementary Reader in English,* is a book of simple reading selections for the beginning student. *Easy Reading Selections in English* is for use on the intermediate level, and *Modern Short Stories* is for the advanced student. If the material in it proves to be too difficult for some classes, it is suggested that one of the two easier readers be tried. For a grammar supplement to this book, the author's *Graded Exercises in English* is suggested.

ROBERT J. DIXSON

MODERN SHORT STORIES IN

ENGLISH

A NEW REVISED EDITION

 Regents Publishing Company, Inc.

Cover design: Paul Gamarello
Text design: Suzanne Bennett & Associates
Illustrations: Connie Maltese

ISBN 0-88345-539-0

Published by Regents Publishing Company, Inc.
2 Park Avenue
New York, New York 10016

Printed in the United States of America

10   9   8   7   6   5   4   3

Contents

Unit 1: My Best Friend

Karen Tucker White

From the time I was a young girl, I had problems with friends. All my girlfriends had "best friends," but I didn't. I never had one special person who always walked home from school with me or called me late at night to talk about things like music or clothes (or later, boys).

My parents used to say that I was a loner, a person who chose her friends carefully, who felt most comfortable when she was alone. It wasn't true. I was never comfortable being alone. I always wished that I had a close friend, like the other kids in my class. Janet Mullaney and Anne Kozach were close friends all through the sixth and seventh grades. How I envied them!

By the time I got to high school, I really began to worry. I knew that I wasn't stupid or ugly or clumsy or any of the other things that kids made fun of, but I still didn't have a special friend that I could share my secret thoughts with.

Occasionally I walked to school with the boy who lived next door. He was my age, so we were in the same grade in school. When we were little, I thought he was gross. I guess that's what all little girls think of all little boys when they're young. Boys are gross, dumb, and dirty. It makes me laugh to think that that's what we thought, but it's true. Doug and I walked to school together, and when he didn't have band practice, we also walked home together, but he didn't count as a friend. He couldn't take the place of a girl my age who felt all the same things I was feeling.

The fact that I didn't have any close girlfriends also seemed to influence my relationships with boys. When I reached my third year of high school, my junior year, all the other girls in the school began to date boys—all except me, that is. I was still a loner.

Now the problem seemed worse. Janet was best friends with a girl named Diane, whom she talked to on the phone for hours. They talked about the boys they liked, they gossiped, they did homework together. Anne had a steady boyfriend, but she had a lot of girls as friends, too, whom she could talk to about all the problems of being sixteen years old. I still had only Doug Thomas, the boy next door. And that didn't count.

I think of my best friend problem as a mountain that I began climbing when I was young. It was a long, hard climb, and I seemed to reach the top of it near the end of my junior year.

The time came for the Junior Prom and I didn't have a date. All of my friends—I guess I should call them acquaintances— were going to this important dance. Of course, they were all talking to their best friends about it. But not only didn't I have anyone to go with, I didn't even have anyone to talk to about it.

My mother told me that she hadn't gone to her Junior Prom either, but I'm not sure she was telling the truth. I think she told me that so I wouldn't feel bad. I felt bad anyway.

I felt so bad that I told Doug about it the next chance I got. He said that he didn't have a date either, and that if neither of us found someone to go with, we could always go to the prom with each other.

2

And that's what happened. Doug and I went to the Junior Prom together. I went because I was embarrassed to stay home, not because I liked Doug. Doug went with me because the girl he liked was already going with someone else. Doug didn't act depressed, and the fact was that we had a pretty good time.

We were invited to a couple of parties after the dance, and then later that week a few acquaintances asked me if I'd like to come to a party they were having. They made it obvious that they wanted me to bring Doug.

I had never paid too much attention to sports in high school, so I didn't know that Doug was now a star swimmer on the school's team. I asked him to go to the party with me and he accepted.

We had a great time at the party, as people crowded around us or joked with us or made references to future events which they hoped we would attend. The attention took me by surprise, but I loved it, since I had never had so many people who wanted to talk to me before.

The new phenomenon continued during the following weeks. Janet called me one day and asked if I wanted to go shopping with her. We had an exhausting yet exhilarating day at the mall and when we got back, she asked me to spend the night at her house. We sat up until 2 A.M. talking about all sorts of things.

A few weeks later, Anne and I worked on a school project together, and I soon realized that I had a couple of "best friends." I was ecstatic.

In the meantime, I went out with Doug a few times. Neither of us was romantically interested in the other, but the other kids in school assumed that we were serious about each other. I liked him, but I was much more interested in my new girlfriends.

Over the summer vacation that year, several events occurred which shook me and my newly found confidence.

Janet and her family moved to another state. We had become good friends by then, and we promised to write and to stay in touch, but we both knew that we probably would never see each other again.

Anne dropped out of school and married her steady boyfriend. She got a job at a local department store, so I see her from time to time; but our interests are different now, so we don't call each other too often.

3

Doug went to summer swimming camp and fell in love with a girl there. She was a swimmer, too, so they had a lot in common. He dates her now, instead of me, but it's OK. I like her, and they make a pretty good couple.

I'm in my senior year, and my problem of having a best friend doesn't seem so insurmountable to me. I have several girlfriends in whom I confide my secrets. Sometimes I visit them, and sometimes they visit me. It all seems so easy and natural that I wonder what I was so worried about.

When I decided to write this, I analyzed all the events and all my thoughts and came to understand something important. I needed help in being able to get close to people. The help came because Doug was popular. It's an odd way for someone to find friends, perhaps, but at least it worked.

I learned something else, too. All the time I was looking for a best friend, I already had one—Doug. About once a week now, without any special plan, we find a way to walk to school together, as we did in the old days. We talk about all the things that are on our minds, complain about our problems, wonder about the future, remember the past. In other words, we're best friends.

Comprehension

1. Why did the narrator of the story want a "best friend"?
2. How did her parents respond to her difficulties?
3. Whom did she walk to school with in her first years of high school? What was her relationship with this person?
4. During her third year of high school, what happened to the narrator's friendships with Janet and Anne?
5. What was her problem at the time of the Junior Prom? How was it solved?
6. Why did people invite her to parties during the weeks following the dance?
7. When did Janet and Anne become her friends? How did it happen?
8. What happened during the summer between the narrator's junior and senior years?
9. At what point in her life is the story being written? What is her attitude toward friendship?
10. What is her relationship with Doug like at the end of the story?

4

Exercises

A. Use each of the following terms in a sentence:
best friend, loner, to envy, clumsy, gross, band, to reach something or someplace, steady boyfriend or girlfriend, to make reference to, to stay in touch, to fall in love, to confide in, in other words.

B. Match the term in the left column with its OPPOSITE in the right column.

Example: _c_ **6.** clumsy   **c.** graceful

___ **1.** close	**a.** stranger
___ **2.** stupid	**b.** obscure
___ **3.** ecstatic	**c.** graceful
___ **4.** acquaintance	**d.** easy
___ **5.** obvious	**e.** past
___ **6.** clumsy	**f.** distant
___ **7.** tell the truth	**g.** smart
___ **8.** future	**h.** lie
___ **9.** from time to time	**i.** depressed
___ **10.** insurmountable	**j.** often

C. The prefix *re-* with verbs means *again.*

He didn't do his work correctly, so he had to do it again.
He had to *redo* it.

Add the prefix *re-* to each verb. Then use the word in a sentence.

Example: redesign   The car didn't work well, so the company had to *redesign* it.

1. design	**6.** tell
2. model	**7.** fill
3. arrange	**8.** settle
4. appear	**9.** build
5. consider	**10.** write

Discussion

1. Do you think it's a good idea for people to have "best friends"?

2. Do you have (or have you had) a best friend? What do (did) you talk about with this person?

3. Name some of the ways in which people become friends. How have you made friends throughout your life?
4. What was the difference, for the narrator of the story, between having girls as friends and having boys as friends? What is the difference for you?
5. Do you think it is easier for sports stars to make friends than for other people? Why? What makes a person popular?

Unit 2: To Love and to Honor

Octavus Roy Cohen

It was rather surprising to discover a deep vein of sentiment in little George Potter. I had been his friend and his lawyer for many years and had watched the always fat and once alert little man settle into a domestic routine. He had been moderately successful in business, sufficiently successful to permit him to retire from it and to travel about the world a little if he had wanted to do so. But instead, he and his present wife, Esther, were content to sit night after night in their pleasant and comfortable living room. She kept busy with her hobby of refinishing old furniture, while he passed the time reading or working on his excellent collection of postage stamps.

Looking back over the years of my friendship with Potter, I can see that the vein of romance had probably been there all the time. There was, for instance, his very romantic love affair with Althea Deane—an affair which almost became a scandal. But just when people began to gossip about them, George married her.

That marriage appeared to extinguish George Potter's last spark of romanticism. It never had a chance to be successful, and when Althea left him suddenly, George's friends thought that he was fortunate to lose her. Later came the news of Althea's death while living abroad, and a couple of years later George began to call upon Esther seriously. The people of our group were only slightly interested; it is difficult to become greatly excited over a possible marriage when both the man and the woman are equally dull and uninteresting.

The marriage was a very nice affair. There followed the usual series of parties for the newly married couple. Then it seemed that George and Esther retired from life. His business affairs ran so well that there was little need on George's part for my services as his lawyer, and while I never ceased to like him, we found less and less in common as the years passed. I couldn't imagine that they were happy; perhaps they were contented, but not really happy. There wasn't enough sentiment; that's the way I figured George. And nothing happened to change my opinion until a few weeks before their twenty-fifth anniversary.

It was then that George came into my office, his fat little face shining with enthusiasm, and he told me of his unusual plan for their silver anniversary. His bright little eyes shone as he explained the thing, and I'll confess that I was pretty well confused; not only because his plan was very sentimental and profoundly impressive, but mainly because it was quiet, dull, old George Potter who was planning this thing—the very George Potter who had lived a quiet life since his second marriage and who had avoided social contacts.

According to what George told me, he was doing this thing for Esther's sake. "It'll please her," he explained. "She likes that sort of thing, you know, and this seems to me a real idea. You have to be a part of it, because you were the best man when Esther and I were married. It's just a gesture on my part—a sort of sacrifice to please her."

I'll say this for George; he didn't do things halfway. Instead of the usual party, he presented a perfect duplication of his marriage to Esther twenty-five years before. There was even the same minister—very old now—and the same violinist who had played "Oh, Promise Me" at the other ceremony. A good many of the original guests were there, most of us rather gray-haired now. But the thing was very impressive: Esther in the same bridal dress she had worn twenty-five years before—let out around the hips, perhaps—and carrying a bouquet of bridal roses; the bridesmaids in pink, with bouquets of Killarney roses; even a person to carry the ring. It was great fun and very impressive, whereas one might have expected it to be absurd.

As for Esther, I never saw a woman look more beautiful. She took on an aura of genuine beauty. Of course, she would have been less than human had she failed to respond to this magnificent exhibition of husbandly devotion. George himself was as frightened as he had been on the occasion of their first wedding.

But finally the ceremony was finished, and the guests went to the dining room for the rich supper which had been prepared by special cooks employed for this occasion. George and I were left alone and he sank, exhausted, into a chair. I placed my hand on his shoulder and congratulated him on the success of his party.

"Do you really think it was a success?" he asked hesitatingly. I noticed some wariness in his eyes.

"It was wonderful!" I responded, and I added jokingly, "And you certainly should feel completely married." I expected a short laugh in return, but received none.

"Yes, I do." He became silent for a moment or two. When he spoke again, his tone was deeply serious. "There's something I want to explain to you both as my friend and as my lawyer." He stopped for a moment and then looked up with a curious expression on his face. "You remember my first wife?"

"Althea?" I was surprised by the question. "Yes, of course."

His voice was strange. "Did you know that she died only last year?"

"Good Lord! Are you certain? I thought she died twenty-seven years ago."

"So did I," he said quietly, looking at me long and pensively. "So did I. I thought I was a widower when I married Esther. I only recently discovered that I wasn't. Don't ask me for details, I don't know any. All I know is that Althea didn't die until August of last year. As far as I know, there are no legal compli-

9

cations, but I wanted you to know in case anything ever comes up. I want you to understand that the affair you attended today was a real wedding for Esther and me."

Comprehension

1. What was George Potter like? What was his relationship with the narrator?
2. What did George and Esther do to pass the time?
3. What was George's relationship with Althea Deane? How did it end?
4. Why weren't George's friends very interested in his relationship with Esther?
5. How did the narrator feel about George over the years?
6. What plan did George make for his twenty-fifth wedding anniversary? Why did this seem unusual to his lawyer?
7. Describe the ceremony. What was special about the minister and the violinist?
8. How did George and Esther react to the ceremony?
9. What was George's manner as he told his friend the real reason for the wedding ceremony?
10. What was that reason?

Exercises

A. Use each of the following terms in a sentence:
rather, to do so, to keep busy, to pass the time, looking back, romance, scandal, to become excited over, in common, to do something halfway, impressive, as for, wariness, complication, in case.

B. Circle the term in parentheses which correctly completes the sentence.

Example: One generally buys stamps in a (bookstore/ post office /movie theater/grocery store).

1. If you were involved in a scandal, you would probably be (happy/in a hurry/embarrassed/sleepy).
2. A bouquet is made of (stones/groceries/stamps/flowers).
3. They were talking about other people. They were (leaving/planning/gossiping/settling down).
4. I never ceased to like him. I never (started/avoided/continued/stopped) liking him.

10

5. There was some wariness in his eyes. He was being (cautious/ecstatic/impressive/ugly).
6. A domestic routine is one which takes place mostly at (the office/home/the swimming pool/a restaurant).
7. A person whose face is shining with enthusiasm is probably (sad/happy/sick/exhausted).
8. A curious expression is a (handsome/shy/dull/strange) expression.
9. If something comes up, it (dies/avoids/stops/arises).
10. To change one's opinion is to change one's (clothes/furniture/ideas/services).

C. The endings *-or* and *-er* are used with some verbs to form nouns, indicating a person or an agent that performs the action of the original verb.

> She illustrates magazines.
> She is an *illustrator* who draws for magazines.
>
> He waits on tables in that restaurant.
> He's a *waiter.*

Change the following verbs to nouns by adding *-or* or *-er*. Then use each word in a sentence.

Example: painter   He went to art school and became a
                    painter.

1. paint	6. collect
2. act	7. educate
3. sing	8. advise
4. govern	9. instruct
5. employ	10. think

Discussion

1. How does your (or your parents') life style compare to that of George and Esther Potter?
2. What do you think the narrator meant when he referred to George's *spark of romanticism?* Do you think of yourself as a romantic person?
3. What legal complications might there have been had Althea returned from abroad after George married Esther?
4. What are wedding ceremonies like in your family?
5. What do you think was going through George's mind as he "remarried"?

Unit 3: New Applications

Chandlee Stokes

Miriam Storley left the bank at 4:15 exactly. People along Division Street said you could set your watch by Miriam; she always left her job at the First State Bank of Cannon Falls at this hour, Monday through Friday, except on holidays. On Fridays she returned to work the six-to-eight P.M. shift. On this particular day, a Monday, she stopped after closing the front door to the bank in order to look at the window display.

Miriam had spent the better part of the afternoon arranging gift items in the bank's window. First State, which is how everyone in town referred to the bank, was having a promotion in order to attract new business. They were offering gifts which ranged in value all the way from a pocket calculator to a color TV. The value of a new depositor's gift depended on how much was initially deposited.

The display in the window was attractive, but Miriam wondered where the new business was going to come from. Cannon Falls wasn't a one-stoplight town, but it wasn't a great metropolis either. There just weren't that many people to warrant an extravagant new business promotion such as this. The bank manager, Al Gropin, had even invested in some full-page advertisements in the local paper and had hired some clowns to perform on the street in front of the bank—all to try to attract new customers.

But Miriam didn't linger long in front of the window, and she didn't waste much time on her thoughts of Al's grand schemes. Her mission today was the same as it had been every weekday for the past several weeks.

She nodded at passersby, shopkeepers, and neighbors as she walked purposefully along the wide sidewalk toward The Computer Shack. There was a pleasant expression on her face as she smiled and said her "hellos" and "good afternoons" and "how are yous" to the people she saw almost every day of her life. Her daily meeting with Officer Quanbeck never failed to amuse her. She smiled to herself as they exchanged greetings and wondered whether he would feel as stupid as he looked after she pulled off the crime of the century.

"Right on time, as usual, eh, Mrs. Storley?" The thin, kindly-looking man behind the counter in The Computer Shack seemed to have a perpetual smile on his face. Every day for the past several weeks, Tobe Barksdale had a short, simple conversation with this woman from the bank down the street. She said she wanted to buy the home computer which he had hooked up to a printer and which was fully operational, but so far all she did was sit and play with it.

Tobe didn't mind the intrusion, though. Even though he opened his shop, gleamingly filled with electronic toys and machines, at noon, the majority of his customers came after six P.M. At first, he had closed the store at eight, but the numbers of people interested in the latest gadgetry forced him to stay open later and later, and now he wasn't closing until ten o'clock.

He could have insisted that his daily visitor make up her mind

13

about the computer, or at least stop using the same program all the time, but she wasn't really any bother, and lately she had acquired such a solid knowledge of the field that he actually enjoyed her increasingly complex questions. She challenged his imagination, probing to see just how far a computer could go, just how much a simple machine could do.

Tobe probably knew as much about computer hardware and software as anybody in the entire town of Cannon Falls. Hardware and software. These were terms the general public rarely heard when Tobe began working a number of years back. Now, everyone used the terms to refer to the computers themselves and the programs which told the machines and operators what to do.

Miriam Storley had a long way to go to catch up with Tobe in her knowledge of this complex field, but she seemed determined, and Tobe was a patient instructor. Each day she would come to him with a new type of problem, an unusual twist, a tricky flow of information or instructions which she wanted to master. Every day he would guide her through the intricacies of the model which was advertised as the "latest, most technologically advanced home computer ever designed." Every day she would listen and absorb, and then experiment for herself. She brought her own tapes and never seemed to tire of learning, even after a day's work. Tobe believed in leaving people to themselves, so when the lesson was over and Miriam sat at the console, enwrapped in her task at hand, he busied himself in another part of the store.

Miriam's teen-age son, who liked to be called by the nickname Zee, had introduced her to the world of computers through his interest in video games. True, she dealt with computers at the bank every day in her job, but somehow they were just a part of the bank; they didn't touch her.

She learned from her son and, almost by accident—as most great discoveries in the world seem to be—she discovered that the latest version of the home-type computers was actually compatible with the one she worked with in her office at First State.

The idea came to her at the end of a particularly tiring day as she tallied the day's receipts and entered them into her desk-top computer. It was foolproof! She could transfer funds from various accounts which were relatively inactive by tampering with the

14

program. If she did it skillfully enough, she would never be caught. She would set up some fictitious accounts in other banks in the state, transfer funds, disguise herself and go to the other banks in order to withdraw the money, and then return the program to its original condition. No one would ever be able to figure out what she had done or where the money had gone. And even if they did trace it, they would never suspect her. How could they?

She decided not to risk working on the program she needed at home, since Zee might see what she was doing. Tobe Barksdale's shop was the perfect cover, and that pleasant man certainly wouldn't suspect her. He didn't even seem to mind letting her use his floor-model computer.

After months of preparation, Miriam carried out her plan. She called Mr. Gropin to say that she was ill and couldn't come to work. Then she drove to Mankato and Red Wing, disguised, and picked up her money. All went well until she arrived home to find Officer Quanbeck and several others waiting in her living room to arrest her for fraud and bank robbery.

As a kindness, to assuage her curiosity, Tobe Barksdale was there, too. He explained, "Your plan was brilliant, Miriam, and you were an excellent student. Indeed, I taught you almost everything you know. But I didn't teach you everything I know. The computer you worked on recorded everything you did on a master tape which I observed every afternoon after you left. After all, I had to see what kind of progress my pupil was making, didn't I?"

Comprehension

1. When did Miriam Storley finish work every day? What did people say about her punctuality?
2. Why had she arranged the bank's window in a special display?
3. Who was the bank manager? What had he done to promote new business?
4. Who was Officer Quanbeck? When did Miriam see him?
5. What did Miriam do at The Computer Shack every day?
6. Who was Tobe Barksdale? What were his store's hours of operation?
7. How did Miriam get interested in computers?

8. Why did she want to tamper with the bank's program?
9. Where did she go on the day that she called in sick? Why did she need a disguise?
10. How did she get caught?

Exercises

A. Use each of the following terms in a sentence:
to set one's watch by, shift, promotion, extravagant, to waste time, grand scheme, as usual, to hook up, so far, at first, gadgetry, just how far, hardware, software, nickname, by accident, to figure out, curiosity, after all.

B. Many words in English may be used as a verb or noun without any change in form.

The publisher will *print* several thousand copies.
The *print* on this page is small and black.

Use each of the following words in a sentence, first as a verb and then as a noun.

1. bank   6. transfer
2. shift   7. master
3. display   8. touch
4. waste   9. experiment
5. smile   10. disguise

C. Match the term in the left column with one which is SIMI-LAR in the right column.

Example: __e__ 10. shortened name   e. nickname

___ 1. conversation   a. take in
___ 2. disguise   b. make happen
___ 3. absorb   c. add
___ 4. foolproof   d. talk
___ 5. touch   e. nickname
___ 6. pull off   f. cover
___ 7. value   g. test
___ 8. tally   h. worth
___ 9. probe   i. affect
___ 10. shortened name   j. infallible

Discussion

1. Would you like to own a home computer? How would you use it?

16

2. What jobs or functions can today's home computers accomplish?
3. Do you ever play any video games? Which ones? Do you think they have any value?
4. What do you think the next generation of computers will enable us to do?
5. Do you think that in a real-life situation, Miriam would have been caught? What other computer-related crimes are possible?

Unit 4: Art for Heart's Sake

Rube Goldberg

Keith Koppel, private duty nurse to the extraordinarily wealthy Collis P. Ellsworth, was glad to leave his patient's room to answer the door. He had had a tiring morning trying to get Ellsworth to cooperate in his own recovery. As soon as Koppel discovered that the caller was Ellsworth's doctor, he began to complain.

"I can't do a thing with him," he told Dr. Caswell. "He won't take his juice. He doesn't want me to read to him. He hates listening to the radio or watching TV. He doesn't like anything."

Actually, he did like something: his business. The problem was that while he was still a fabulously wealthy man, he had recently begun to make big mistakes. He insisted on buying companies at very high prices, only to watch them fail or go bankrupt.

Ellsworth was in pretty good shape for a 76-year-old, but his business failures were ruinous to his health. He had suffered his last heart attack after his disastrous purchase of a small railroad in Iowa. The health problem he suffered before that came about because of excitement over the failure of a chain of grocery stores, stores which he had purchased at an inflated price. It seemed that all his recent purchases had to be liquidated at a great sacrifice to both his pocketbook and his health. They were beginning to have serious effects.

Dr. Caswell had done his homework, however. He realized that he needed to interest the old man in something which would take his mind off his problem and redirect his energies. His answer was art. The doctor entered his patient's room.

"I hear that you haven't been obeying orders," the doctor said.

"Who's giving me orders at my time of life?"

The doctor drew up his chair and sat down close to the old man. "I've got a suggestion for you," he said quietly.

Old Ellsworth looked suspiciously over his eyeglasses. "What is it, more medicine, more automobile rides, more foolishness to keep me away from my office?"

"How would you like to take up art?" The doctor had his stethoscope ready in case the suddenness of the suggestion proved too much for the patient's heart.

But the old man's answer was a strong "Foolishness!"

"I don't mean seriously," said the doctor, relieved that nothing had happened. "Just play around with chalk and crayons. It'll be fun."

But after several more scowls, which were met with gentle persuasion by the wise doctor, Ellsworth gave in. He would, at least, try it for a while.

Caswell went to his friend Judson Livingston, head of the Atlantic Art Institute, and explained the situation. Livingston produced Frank Swain. Swain was an 18-year-old art student, quite good, who needed money to continue his education. He would tutor Ellsworth one afternoon a week for ten dollars an hour.

Their first lesson was the next afternoon. It was less than an overwhelming success. Swain began by arranging some paper and crayons on the table.

"Let's try to draw that vase over there," he suggested.

"What for? It's only a bowl with some blue stains on it. Or are they green?"

"Try it, Mr. Ellsworth, please."

"Umph!" The old man took a piece of crayon in a shaky hand and drew several lines. He drew several more and then connected these crudely. "There it is, young man," he said with a tone of satisfaction. "Such foolishness!"

Frank Swain was patient. He needed the ten dollars. "If you want to draw, you will have to look at what you're drawing, sir."

Ellsworth looked. "Gosh, it's rather pretty. I never noticed it before."

Koppel came in with the announcement that his patient had done enough for the first lesson.

"Oh, it's pineapple juice again," Ellsworth said. Swain left, not sure if he would be invited back.

When the art student came the following week, there was a drawing on the table that had a slight resemblance to a vase. The wrinkles deepened at the corners of the old gentleman's eyes as he asked, "Well, what do you think of it?"

"Not bad, sir," answered Swain. "But it's not quite straight."

"Gosh," old Ellsworth smiled, "I see. The halves don't match." He added a few lines with a shaking hand and colored the open spaces blue, like a child playing with a picture book. Then he looked towards the door. "Listen, young man," he whispered, "I want to ask you something before old Pineapple Juice comes back."

"Yes, sir," answered Swain politely.

"I was thinking—do you have the time to come twice a week, or perhaps three times?"

As the weeks went by, Swain's visits grew more frequent. When Dr. Caswell called, Ellsworth would talk about the graceful lines of the chimney or the rich variety of color in a bowl of fruit.

The treatment was working perfectly. No more trips downtown to his office for the purpose of buying some business that was to fail later. No more crazy financial plans to try the strength of his tired old heart. Art was a complete cure for him.

20

The doctor thought it safe to allow Ellsworth to visit the Metropolitan Museum, the Museum of Modern Art, and other exhibitions with Swain. An entirely new world opened up its mysteries to him. The old man showed a tremendous curiosity in the art galleries and in the painters who exhibited in them. How were the galleries run? Who selected the pictures for the exhibitions? An idea was forming in his brain.

When the late spring began to cover the fields and gardens with color, Ellsworth painted a simply horrible picture which he called "Trees Dressed in White." Then he made a surprising announcement. He was going to exhibit the picture in the summer show at the Lathrop Gallery.

The summer show at the Lathrop Gallery was the biggest art exhibition of the year—in quality, if not in size. The lifetime dream of every important artist in the United States was a prize from this exhibition. Among the paintings of this distinguished group of artists, Ellsworth was now going to place his "Trees Dressed in White," which resembled a handful of salad dressing thrown violently against the side of a house.

"If the newspapers hear about this, everyone in town will be laughing at Mr. Ellsworth. We've got to stop him," said Koppel.

"No," warned the doctor. "We can't interfere with him now and take a chance of ruining all the good work which we have done."

To the complete surprise of all three—and especially Swain —"Trees Dressed in White" was accepted for the Lathrop show. Not only was Mr. Ellsworth crazy, thought Koppel, but the Lathrop Gallery was crazy, too.

Fortunately, the painting was hung in an inconspicuous place, where it did not draw any special notice or comment.

During the course of the exhibition, the old man kept on taking lessons, seldom mentioning his picture. He was unusually cheerful. Every time Swain entered the room, he found Ellsworth laughing to himself. Maybe Koppel was right. The old man was crazy. But it seemed equally strange that the Lathrop committee should encourage his craziness by accepting his picture.

Two days before the close of the exhibition, a special messenger brought a long, official-looking envelope to Mr. Ellsworth

21

while Swain, Koppel, and the doctor were in the room. "Read it to me," said the old man. "My eyes are tired from painting."

> It gives the Lathrop Gallery great pleasure to announce that the First Prize of $1,000 has been awarded to Collis P. Ellsworth for his painting "Trees Dressed in White."

Swain and Koppel were so surprised that they could not say a word. Dr. Caswell, exercising his professional self-control with a supreme effort, said, "Congratulations, Mr. Ellsworth. Fine, fine. . . . Of course, I didn't expect such great news. But, but— well, now, you'll have to admit that art is much more satisfying than business."

"Art has nothing to do with it," said the old man sharply. "I bought the Lathrop Gallery last month."

Comprehension

1. Who was Keith Koppel? What was his complaint about his patient?
2. What had Collis P. Ellsworth begun doing recently that had his doctor concerned?
3. What did Dr. Caswell prescribe in order to help his patient avoid further health problems?
4. Who was Frank Swain? How did he get the job as tutor?
5. What was the difference between the first Ellsworth drawing of the vase and the second drawing?
6. How often did Ellsworth want Swain to come?
7. What happened when Ellsworth began to visit museums and galleries?
8. What was "Trees Dressed in White"? How good was it?
9. What was the Lathrop Gallery? Why did some people think the Lathrop committee was crazy?
10. What was the final twist to the story?

Exercises

A. Use each of the following terms in a sentence:
   as soon as, to go bankrupt, chain of stores, to be in good shape, to take one's mind off something, to keep away from, in case, to go by, not bad, a handful, salad dressing, to take a chance, official-looking, of course, nothing to do with it.

B. Match the term in the left column with one which has the SAME meaning in the right column.

Example: __i__ 2. dull   **i.** uninteresting

___ 1. wealthy	**a.** unhappy
___ 2. dull	**b.** ended
___ 3. crazy	**c.** continue
___ 4. keep on	**d.** unusually
___ 5. chance	**e.** opportunity
___ 6. extraordinarily	**f.** insane
___ 7. over	**g.** bear
___ 8. sad	**h.** prize
___ 9. stand	**i.** uninteresting
___ 10. award	**j.** rich

C. The prefixes *un-*, *in-*, *im-*, *il-*, and *dis-* are used with adjectives and adverbs to give a negative or opposite meaning.

Give the negative form of each of the following adjectives or adverbs. Then use the word in a sentence.

Example: uninteresting   This book is too *uninteresting* to finish.

1. interesting	6. loyal
2. patiently	7. honest
3. agreeable	8. sure
4. able	9. attentive
5. legal	10. politely

Discussion

1. In what other ways could a person in Mr. Ellsworth's condition have redirected his energies?
2. Have you ever produced any artwork? What kind?
3. What are some ways in which people of all ages can stay in shape? What do you do to get or stay in shape?
4. Do you enjoy going to art museums? Which ones have you visited?
5. What is the purpose of an art exhibition?

Unit 5: That Restless Feeling

Peg Grady

Mrs. Feldmeyer found her in her bedroom crying. She stood in the doorway and said seriously, "I came over to borrow your vacuum cleaner, Carolyn. Mine's broken. The door was open, so I just walked in. What on earth is the matter?"

Carolyn sat up and dried her eyes. She was embarrassed that Mrs. Feldmeyer had come in while she was crying. She had been caught letting her emotions get the better of her. She shook her head to control herself. "Nothing. Really. I'm OK. Of course you may borrow the vacuum. It's in the closet. I'll get it." She rose shakily.

Mrs. Feldmeyer put her hands on her hips, cocked her head,

and looked skeptical. "Nothing, eh? It's because Joe wants to leave Libertyville, isn't it? Of course it is."

Carolyn pushed her thinning blond hair out of her eyes and said, somewhat defiantly, "I won't do it. I won't."

"He's got that restless feeling, hasn't he? I've known that boy since he was a little tyke. I guess a person could see it coming. This is a small town, and a fellow like Joe Conly gets restless and needs to get out into the world. I don't think you're going to have too much luck trying to fight an urge like that one, my dear."

"But I don't have the urge. I won't move from town to town all my life. I like it here. I know everyone. It's peaceful. I don't have to worry about things. Well, I do worry about some things, but you know what I mean. It's like an old pair of slippers. They're comfortable. Why would I want to buy a new pair?"

"Carolyn, you married Joe for better or worse. He's got something inside him that says, 'Get out there on the road.' Now how are you going to deal with that?"

"I don't know," she said, her head bowed slightly.

"Of course you don't. You're just a child. You'll fight it and fight it and the next thing you know, twenty years will have passed, and by then it will be too late to do any good. Unless you find someone to tell you what to do to begin with. Someone who knows."

Carolyn was still depressed. "Who could know the answer, Mrs. Feldmeyer? Who could tell me what to do? I've argued and reasoned with Joe until I'm almost crazy, but he doesn't even listen anymore. His mind is made up. He says that I could find another job easily with my talents, and that this is something he needs to do."

"Is he right? About you finding another job easily, that is?"

"I suppose so. That's not the part I'm upset about. I'd like to take a few years off from work anyway. You know, when we have children. I've always thought that it would be great to stay home and be with the children for a few years. Until they're in school. It's just that I've never wanted to travel. I always thought that we'd live a quiet, uncomplicated life right here in dull little Libertyville, but Joe seems so restless."

"Like Mr. Feldmeyer."

25

Carolyn looked up, surprised. "You mean Mr. Feldmeyer used to . . . wanted to . . . ?"

"He was the hardest man to hold in this town. He was aching to get on the road. Just like your Joe. But he stayed. He stayed all his life, God bless him."

"Why?" Carolyn asked. "What did you do?"

"I always gave in. It worked, too."

Carolyn looked confused and disappointed. "Oh."

"But he didn't know it. Oh, I suppose you could call what I did 'being manipulative,' but we were a happy pair, we were. He got his way and I got mine. 'Course, I don't know if what I did would work with your Joe."

"Well, at least tell me about it. What did you do? What do you mean, you 'gave in'? How could you get your way by giving in?"

"Whenever Mr. Feldmeyer got that restless feeling, I always took him on a trip. Just for a week or two. And I kept him jumping every minute of those trips. I never minded short vacations anyway; they were fun. Well, by the time that man would get home, he'd be so tired of jumping around from place to place, he wouldn't have left Libertyville for a million dollars."

"Oh, I don't think that would be right. It would be like tricking Joe. And besides, it probably wouldn't work."

"Maybe it wouldn't. I'm the last person in the world to try to tell folks how to live their lives, Carolyn, but it seems to me that you're pretty unhappy right now. You're going to have to do something to solve this problem you and Joe have. Why not give it a try. Tell him you'd like to take a short vacation before you change your life style."

They did it. They left Tennessee and headed east, stopping in Louisville and Lexington in Kentucky and then wandering north through Cincinnati, Columbus, and Dayton, Ohio, and then back west through Indianapolis before coming back by way of Nashville. They were gone seven days. Each day they rose at dawn and got on the road, stopping at every historical marker and tourist attraction they saw. Carolyn planned almost every moment, filling each with some purposeful activity. She also filled Joe with fast food and stale coffee, remarking that that was all they had time to eat since their main goal was to see as much as they could. Joe's enthusiasm began to wane on the third day out. A lifeless cloud began to cover his eyes.

Mrs. Feldmeyer dropped over the day after they returned to bring back the vacuum cleaner she had borrowed. Joe was still asleep, but Carolyn was up getting ready for work.

Carolyn's news was "good," but there was an odd quality to her voice as she told it. "About halfway through the trip, Joe stopped talking about going on the road," she related. "He hasn't said a word for days about being restless. He says he's anxious to get back to work at the plant. He's even suggested that we invite his brother and his family to visit us this Christmas instead of going to Chicago to visit them, as we had planned."

"I'll bet he said that home never looked so good to him, too."

"Exactly. I probably won't even be able to get him to go to a movie for a month." Carolyn managed a slight smile.

"You look tired, dear, not too happy, and more than a little weary."

"Weary? Yes, I suppose I am. Weary of this town and this life. I never knew how old and dull and tiresome this town was. I thought we'd spend our entire lives here. I wanted to have a family and have a life for my children just like the life I had. But now . . ."

Mrs. Feldmeyer looked at Carolyn seriously for a moment. "You're just tired from the trip, dear. I'll bet all that traveling was a strain on you. It was such a long trip . . ."

"It wasn't the travel." When Carolyn looked up, her eyes were different. They were shining with a new life and vibrancy she had never felt before. "The trip was exciting. I had a wonderful time!"

Comprehension

1. Why did Mrs. Feldmeyer visit Carolyn at the beginning of the story?
2. What was Carolyn doing when Mrs. Feldmeyer arrived? Why?
3. Who was Joe Conly? What did he want to do?
4. Why did Carolyn want to stay in Libertyville?
5. What did she want to do when she had children?
6. What was Mrs. Feldmeyer's advice?

27

7. Where did Carolyn and Joe go on their short vacation?
8. How did they spend their time on the vacation?
9. What was Joe's reaction to their week on the road?
10. Describe the change that came over Carolyn while on vacation.

Exercises

A. Use each of the following terms in a sentence:
what on earth, to be the matter, to get the better of, to be OK, to cock one's head, defiantly, tyke, for better or worse, to deal with, almost crazy, to be upset about something, manipulative, fast food, tourist attraction, on the road.

B. Supply the appropriate tag ending for each of these sentences.

Example: You're going, _____?
      You're going, aren't you?

1. It's because he wants to leave, _____?
2. He wants to move, _____?
3. You're tired from your trip, _____?
4. I don't have to leave this town, _____?
5. She decided to work for a while, _____?
6. The vacuum cleaner is in the closet, _____?
7. She wasn't tired from her trip, _____?
8. They've already left for Chicago, _____?
9. We can't go on vacation with you this year, _____?
10. You're not crying because you're happy, _____?

C. The opposite of the *-ful* ending for adjectives is *-less*, which has the general meaning of *without*. Change the following nouns to adjectives, first by adding *-ful* and then by adding *-less*. Then use each word in a sentence.

Example: restful   We had a *restful* vacation.
          restless   I'm too *restless* to take a long car trip.

1. rest		6. event
2. care		7. use
3. pity		8. thought
4. grace		9. fear
5. hope		10. color

28

Discussion

1. Do you think you would enjoy living "on the road"? What do you think it would be like?
2. What do you think of the way in which Mrs. Feldmeyer and Carolyn manipulated their husbands? Was it unfair?
3. What are the advantages of living in a small town? The disadvantages?
4. Do you ever get a restless feeling? What do you do about it?
5. Where did you go on your last vacation? Was it rushed? What kind of food did you eat? How did you feel when you returned home?

Unit 6: Last Call

Walter Davenport

Most people would have told young Sherrill the facts at the beginning, using no more words than were necessary for simple courtesy.

But that wasn't Ham's way.

Ham Mason probably would have been a good public speaker if he had wanted to. He truly loved to talk. Ham was content, however, to run his small hotel in Owensboro. He owned the Mason House, was its general repairman, and could usually be found at its front desk chatting with anyone and everyone who wandered by.

"Glad to have you, Mr. Sherrill. Will you be staying with us a few days?" Sherrill had rented a car and driven in from the airport. He had made his reservation at the Mason House by mail weeks ago.

"A few days, at least, Mr. . . . ?"

"Mason. I'm the proprietor. Everyone 'round here calls me Ham, though. Let me see." Ham looked at the board where, in great disarray, hung the keys to the various rooms. "Four, five, six, se— I can let you have number six. It's got a desk in it, if you think you'll want to do some work. I notice you've got a hefty briefcase there."

Ham talked all the while Mr. Sherrill filled out the registration card. He talked as they walked down the hall to Sherrill's room, and he talked as he opened the curtains in the room, letting in the last rays of the setting sun. Ham instinctively knew that young people were durable about listening to him, whereas an older person might have silenced him minutes ago.

"From New York, you say? What's your business?"

"Investments," said the young businessman. "I'm with Chaffee and Bates, one of the oldest investment houses in New York. I haven't been with them long. I guess that's why they sent me out chasing old business, trying to make new business out of it. I've come to see Mr. Edward Colesberry. Do you know him?"

A true orator takes advantage of any opportunity. Ham saw a real chance to exhibit his gifts of eloquence.

"Ed Colesberry?" he almost shouted, "Why, Mr. Sherrill, there's no one in this whole town who could tell you he was closer to him. So you came all the way from New York City to see Ed Colesberry, eh?" Ham was warming up to his newly found audience and was very pleased with himself.

"Him and a few others," said the young man. "Mr. Colesberry used to do business with us, but he hasn't for a while. The firm decided to send out us new fellows to look up old customers."

"Well, I don't plan to take up too much of your valuable time, young fellow, but if you'd like, I could tell you something about this man you've come so far to see."

Sherrill was eager to hear and learn something about Ed Colesberry, so he joined Ham in the hotel dining room for a cup of coffee while the hotel man, elated with his audience, began his tale.

"Ed Colesberry was seventy years old last month. Getting along in years. He and I went to school together, so you know that I knew him well all my life. Popular boy, Ed was. Smart,

31

too. Half the businessmen in town wanted Ed to work for them when he graduated from high school.

" 'Ham,' Ed said to me the day after graduation, 'I'm going to work for Willis Deemer for a while. Then as soon as I get some money saved, I'm going to New York to do some big things with my life. I'm not going to bury myself here in Owensboro. I'm not going to be happy until I hear the flight announcer over the loudspeaker saying, "Last call for Trans-Global's flight to New York City!" '

"Well, Ed worked in Willis Deemer's hardware store for a year and did so well that Deemer, who was getting ready to retire, offered to make Ed a partner. Ed said no several times to that offer, when all of a sudden, Deemer died. Willis's widow begged Ed to stay on and take over the business for a while because it was all that Willis had left to her.

"Ed stayed a little longer, all the while thinking that he didn't want to be tied down, but soon the Deemer hardware store was the biggest in the county and getting bigger. Meanwhile, Ed fell in love with Maureen Brent, whose father had the area's largest real estate operation.

"Ed and Maureen planned to marry and then move to New York, where he still planned to be 'someone.' He used to tell her that he couldn't wait to hear that announcement: 'Last call for the flight to New York.'

"Well, Sherrill, Maureen got sick, so they postponed the wedding a few times, and when they did get married, her doctor told them they shouldn't move so close to the ocean as New York, at least not for a year or so.

"So they stayed in Owensboro, getting richer at the store but still planning to go to New York at any cost. Next thing you know, Ed and Maureen had a baby and Maureen's father talked Ed into taking over one of his real estate projects. It made them a great deal of money, so they decided to hold onto Ed's dream but to delay it for a few years. It seemed that everything Ed touched turned to gold in those days. The project got bigger and bigger and everyone trusted Ed. Owensboro probably never had a bigger moneymaker than that project and Ed Colesberry.

"Wouldn't you know it? The next thing that happened was that Maureen's father died, and Ed had to take over the entire company. He was madder than a bear, and he had had enough.

He sold half his interest in everything he owned, made arrangements for others to run the businesses, and tried to sell his house.

"They had a second child by then, but he and Maureen were ready to leave for New York at last. 'Ham,' Ed said to me, 'I'm going to New York. Yes, sir. The time has come. Maureen is still somewhat ill, so she'll need special doctors that are only in New York. I want to send the kids to fine schools, too. Yes sir, soon I'll be hearing that announcement: "Last call" that announcer will say.'

"Well, Mr. Sherrill, just at that time Tom Staub, the cashier at the savings bank, ran off with all the money and the bank almost failed completely. The people in town had lost most of their money and they wanted someone to come to their rescue and save the bank. You can guess whom they turned to, can't you? Ed Colesberry.

"Maureen herself wanted to go to New York by that time, but she persuaded Ed to step in even though he never had any banking experience. Of course it took a little time, but Ed saved it.

"He came out of it president of the bank. It's the biggest savings bank in this end of the state today. But when Ed took over that bank he came to me and said that no matter what happened, he was going to New York and nobody could stop him. I couldn't help laughing a little."

Ham paused impressively.

"So I'll find him at the savings bank, then?" said young Sherrill.

"No, you won't. Ed finally made it to New York. I was coming to that part, even though it's taken me a while. Ed died last week. In his will, which he made right after they made him president of the bank, he left a million dollars to the town (with the rest of his sizable estate going to his wife and children) provided that they bury him in New York. He was determined to get there somehow."

Comprehension

1. What did Ham Mason do for a living?
2. Who was Sherrill? How did he get to Owensboro?
3. Why had Sherrill's firm sent him there?
4. Why was Ham eager to talk to Sherrill?

5. What was Ham's relationship to Ed Colesberry? How well do you think the two men knew each other? Why?
6. What was Colesberry's dream?
7. Who was Maureen Brent? How many children did she and her husband have?
8. Why did Ed take over the hardware store business? How did the business do?
9. What jobs did Ed have after working at the hardware store? How did he do in each job?
10. How did Ed finally get to New York? How does this relate to the title of the story?

Exercises

A. Use each of the following terms in a sentence:
public speaker, reservation, hefty, setting sun, to silence someone, to warm up to, a while, last call, all of a sudden, to stay on, to take over, to be tied down, a year or so, to turn to gold, to turn to someone, even though, to step in.

B. Circle the term in parentheses which best completes the sentence.

Example: A (vase/desk/briefcase/envelope) is used to hold flowers.

1. Most men's shoes are tied with (handkerchiefs/laces/vests/boots).
2. Most pants are worn with a (sleeve/cuff/belt/necktie).
3. When a window is shut, it is (open/clean/broken/closed).
4. I park my car in a parking (lot/highway/room/station).
5. My (nose/chin/forehead/collar) is not a part of my face.
6. A strong-willed person has (education/determination/physical strength/a disease).
7. You probably would not be able to buy a (screwdriver/hammer/curtain/box of nails) in a hardware store.
8. A real estate salesperson sells (fruit/cars/beds/houses).
9. A million dollars is $(1,000/1,000,000,000/1,000,000/100).
10. They talked Ed into it; in other words, they (persuaded/narrated/orated/spoke) him.

C. Fill in the missing form of the word.

Example: ___curiosity___ _____ _____
(___curiosity___ ___curious___ ___curiously___)

Noun	Adjective	Adverb
1. _____	courteous	_____
2. contentment	_____	_____
3. _____	_____	intelligently
4. _____	_____	durably
5. _____	serious	_____
6. value	_____	_____
7. anger	_____	_____
8. _____	eloquent	_____
9. _____	_____	silently
10. warmth	_____	_____

Discussion

1. Do you know any people who, like Ham Mason, like to talk a lot? What are they like? Are you ever like that?
2. What is an investment house? What does someone like Sherrill do for a living?
3. What do you imagine was the secret of Ed Colesberry's success?
4. Do you have a will? Do you think it's a good idea to have one? To whom would you leave your possessions?
5. Do you have any dreams similar to Ed's? What are they?

Unit 7: Red Balloons

Elmer Davis

After it happened, Lundy told himself that the temptation had been too great. In fact, he had never been truly tempted before, for the opportunity had never arisen. He had gone to the bank —the branch bank in the poor, run-down neighborhood to which he had recently moved—to review his dwindling investments and savings. He had recently lost a great deal of his financial security in a crazy attempt to make money by playing the stock market so that he could give up his job and live in Florida. He took his safe-deposit box to one of the booths where people shut themselves in while they open their boxes in order to put in or remove valuables. The booth had just been vacated by a fat woman wearing many jewels who had left it covered with torn papers.

A little annoyed, Lundy brushed away the torn papers—and came upon an envelope filled with money which the fat woman had obviously overlooked. The recent recession had frightened many people; the fat woman looked like the sort of person who would turn her bank balance into cash and lock it up in her safe-deposit box. Lundy half opened the door to call her back and saw her walking out of the bank. Quickly he shut the door and counted the money. Nearly ninety thousand dollars; enough to keep a man comfortably in some little Florida town for the rest of his life.

Quickly, Lundy slipped the envelope into his inside pocket.

Then he left the bank, crossing the street into a little park with a high iron fence around it. It was, he knew, a private park, the possession of the old families that had once lived on the square; at night its gates were locked and a watchman guarded it. But by day it was open to all. He sat down on a bench, trembling in the winter wind; the envelope in his pocket felt like a piece of hot metal.

What a fool he had been! He had thought when he took it that it wouldn't be missed for a month—not until the woman came again to get something else. But if she kept all her money in her safe-deposit box she might come back and find it missing tomorrow—or even this afternoon. The bank employees would remember Lundy, as he had recently rented his safe-deposit box; they might remember that he had followed her into the booth. If he gave up his job now and left for Florida, that would be a confession. But tonight, tomorrow, he might be questioned, his rooms examined. Where could he hide the money?

His throat was dry. He got up and walked to the center of the park, where he had seen a drinking fountain. Unable to decide what to do, he stared at the fountain, at its tall concrete base. Then his eyes narrowed; the base was broken on one side and had a hole big enough to put your hand through. Inside, there was a dark space where no one would think of looking for anything; where a man who had hidden something could come back and get it almost anytime.

Beside the drinking fountain, Lundy knelt down; anyone who had passed would have seen only a man with an unbuttoned overcoat hanging loose about him, kneeling down, tying his shoe. But when he went on, the envelope of money no longer lay like a piece of hot metal in his pocket. He had hidden it in the hole at the base of the drinking fountain.

That evening two detectives from police headquarters came

37

to see him, to question him very politely, and he met them smiling.

"Yes, yes," he said. "There was a fat woman in the booth just before me; she left it covered with torn pieces of paper and I brushed them aside into the wastepaper basket. Find out where the basket went, and you'll probably find the money. . . . No, I've no objection at all if you want to look around here just to satisfy yourselves."

Afterward he wondered whether he had not overdone it. They went away apparently convinced, but he couldn't feel safe. He had better leave the money where it was, for a while. There wasn't a chance in a million that anyone would look into the broken drinking fountain. There was no hope of his recovering the money at night: The park gate was locked, and the watchman was on duty. Someday, when no one was near, he would kneel down as if to tie his shoe . . .

As he entered the park the next morning, he saw something like a red cloud just above the drinking fountain. A red warning of danger. He became very nervous but then saw that it was only a group of toy balloons held by an old man. Lundy had never seen anyone selling balloons here in the three weeks he had lived in the neighborhood. Business couldn't be good for the old man; surely he would leave soon. But when Lundy came that evening, the old man was still in the same spot near the drinking fountain.

Lundy looked at him in passing; he was old, but he looked strong. He might be a younger man in disguise, not a seller of balloons; he might be a detective placed there to watch him. Lundy went home trembling. No one could have seen him put the money away—but suppose that by some accident the money had been found. The police would know the thief must come back for it; thus they had left a man on guard. *But had they left the money there in order to trap him?*

The next morning the balloon-seller was still there. That day Lundy went to the bank and risked a question. No, said the manager of the bank, they hadn't found the money, but they expected to find it. It seemed to Lundy that the manager looked at him in a rather suspicious manner.

That evening he spoke, in passing, to the balloon-seller.

"You work late, eh? Business must be good."

"Not so good. But I stay around until they lock the gates each night and the watchman arrives to guard the place."

There was not a moment when the fountain was not being watched. That was the first night that Lundy could not sleep. In the morning the red cloud was still there, hanging above his treasure.

Well, if business was bad, the balloon-seller would soon leave and go somewhere else to sell his balloons. Lundy waited three more days, in which he saw, morning and evening, that red sign of danger. He couldn't stand this much longer: A balloon-seller, staying in a place where Lundy had never seen one before, couldn't be a balloon-seller. But there was one chance if the police had left the money. Policemen in uniform seldom came here; Lundy could wait for his chance until there was no one around, attack the balloon-seller, knock him out, take the money, and escape before anyone came.

And so he waited for his chance, found the old man alone, walked up to him, pretended to buy a balloon, then hit him straight and hard on the jaw. Down went the old man—down and out; down went Lundy on his knees, his arm reaching into the hole at the base of the fountain.

Up into the air went a dozen red balloons, released from the old man's hand as he fell; a dozen sudden red danger signals which could be seen everywhere in the park and from the nearby streets as well. As Lundy rose, pushing the money into his pocket, he saw a policeman coming up; he turned only to face another, tried to walk away coolly . . .

"Hey!" said the policeman. "What's the matter with old Joe?"

"I don't know. I've done nothing." But the balloon man was talking now, explaining to the policeman what had happened. The policeman turned toward Lundy, severe.

"What's the idea of knocking down an old man that's just out of the hospital?"

"Just out of the hospital?" Lundy asked.

"Sure. He's been sick for a month. Haven't you noticed that for the past month he hasn't been here, at his regular place near the fountain? First time he's been away for twenty years. . . . Here, you—take your hand out of that pocket! Oh, it isn't a gun? Just papers? Well, come along with me and show them to the captain at police headquarters."

39

Comprehension

1. Why did Lundy go to the bank in the run-down neighborhood?
2. What did he discover when he went into the booth? How did he react?
3. Where did Lundy go after he left the bank?
4. What did he decide to do with the money?
5. What was the "red cloud" above the drinking fountain? Why did this alarm Lundy?
6. What did Lundy suspect that the old man might really be? Why?
7. What plan did Lundy formulate?
8. Why did he go back to the bank? What happened?
9. What happened when Lundy attacked the balloon-seller?
10. What did the policeman think was in Lundy's pocket? What did he order Lundy to do?

Exercises

A. Use each of the following terms in a sentence:
run-down, investment, a great deal of, stock market, safe-deposit box, to come upon, to overlook, to give up something, to kneel down, to overdo something, to knock somebody out, to put something away, to wait for, to be the matter with.

B. Circle the term in parentheses which best completes the sentence.

Example: A person who is sick is (well/fat/(ill)/convinced).

1. A man whose duty is to guard a building at night is a (banker/watchman/sergeant/thief).
2. A person who is scared is (relieved/adjusted/balanced/frightened).
3. A (pocket/headquarters/knee/uniform) is part of the body.
4. A thief can also be called a (captain/robber/banker/watchman).
5 To lock something, you need a (key/money/booth/basket).
6. A good place to keep valuable things is a (pillow/hole/drinking fountain/safe-deposit box).

40

7. When you nod, you move your (hand/finger/head/leg) slightly.
8. You use your (finger/elbow/knee/neck) to point.
9. A shop is a (cafeteria / small store / genuine interest / bank).
10. A person with financial trouble has problems with (employees/money/the police/time).

C. A common ending that makes nouns from adjectives is *-ity*.

active—activity
I keep *active* by playing golf. Golf is now my favorite *activity*.

Change the following adjectives to nouns by adding *-ity*. Then use each word in a sentence.

Example: responsibility   She has a job with a lot of *responsibility*.

1. responsible	6. creative
2. capable	7. secure
3. similar	8. original
4. popular	9. obese
5. legal	10. personal

Discussion

1. Have you ever been confronted with a great temptation to do something illegal? What was it like?
2. What do you think happened to Lundy after he went to the police station? What would they have charged him with?
3. Do you, or does anyone you know, have a safe-deposit box? Why are safe-deposit boxes used?
4. What does *playing the stock market* involve? What is a *recession*?
5. What does it mean to *act in a suspicious manner*? What mannerisms do people have which might make them appear guilty of something? Do you think you could hide the fact that you had committed a crime?

Unit 8: Decision

Roy Hilligoss

Even after a year, Tran still called us Aunt Pat and Uncle Andy. We had long since become accustomed to the role of parents, and we assumed that one day we would legally adopt the eight-year-old who was in our care. That was before the letter came from the United Nations Refugee Agency to our home in Fairfax, Virginia, a suburb of Washington, D.C.

Tran had come to us as a refugee from the wars which had been ravaging Southeast Asia for decades. Pat and I had served in the Foreign Service in South Vietnam in the late sixties and then in Kampuchea and Thailand in the seventies and early eighties. We were well acquainted with the suffering of the people of that area—especially of the children.

Tran's parents were alive, but they felt that she would be safer if she went to the United States to live, at least until her homeland became less of a battlefield.

The letter contained news which we had always feared. Tran's parents had been killed in a guerilla raid on their village, which was really an overcrowded camp. Deaths in the camp often came from malnutrition, but this was brutal.

Tran took the news with the slightest show of emotion. We knew that there was a sharp pain in her little heart, but we also knew that she could not show it. Her people were fighting a desperate battle, so she could not let her own individual tragedy supersede the larger one.

"I shall try very hard," she told us in that thin, soft voice, "to be as you would want your own daughter to be. I shall learn American ways as quickly as I can and try to make you proud of me." She managed a weak smile. "I shall even try to admire your history."

We loved Tran and wanted her to stay with us forever. Her sadness was our sadness, and it made us more of a family.

She did well in school. She even reached the finals in a statewide spelling bee. Her accent disappeared, and she became a popular, contributing member of her class in school.

Then a second letter came.

It was from a distant relative of Tran's, one whom she had never met. He was fond of Tran's parents, the letter said, and he would like to offer her a place to live—with his mother. I looked up from the letter. "He says he recognizes the danger of having her return to such a war-torn country, but he thinks Tran would be good company for his mother. She's old and alone. Oh, Pat . . . do you think she'll want to go?"

She shook her head slowly. "I don't know. I've always been afraid that she would leave us one day."

"She doesn't know anyone there anymore. Surely she'd be happier here, with us . . ."

"She's not really ours, Andy. We hoped she would be, and she's tried to pretend, but . . ."

"I know. I was only hoping, not talking sense. Well, let's go up to her room and tell her about this letter."

We watched her glistening brown eyes move quickly back and forth across the page, and when they reached the bottom they stayed there. She was thinking rapidly. Suddenly, I knew she had reached a decision because her face lost all expression—a habit of hers.

"I must go, Aunt Pat, Uncle Andy. It is my duty."

"It is still dangerous. There are bombs. There is hunger and misery."

"That is why I must go."

"I don't understand," I said.

"I mean . . ." for a moment she paused, ". . . well, when your country's having its most difficult times, that's when it needs you the most."

That sounded a bit too grown-up, too much like something she had read somewhere. I looked at her suspiciously, but her eyes did not waver as they met mine bravely. "All right, Tran. If you feel that's what you must do, then of course you shall go. I'm sorry."

"I'm sorry, too."

We stood there awkwardly for a minute, saying nothing. Then Pat said, "I'm bungry," and we all laughed. It was a mispronunciation of *hungry*. Tran had had a hard time with that word when she first arrived in Fairfax. Now it had become a family word to indicate that we should all go fix dinner together.

I was slicing some tomatoes and cucumbers when I began to miss Tran already, in my heart. How quickly one's world can turn upside down. We didn't talk much about her departure, but we might as well have discussed it constantly. From that first night, on through the week following, there were few signs of cheerfulness in our house.

We decided to drive to New York, where there was a nonstop flight. Pat and I arranged to take off from work, and we worked out the final details of Tran's journey. Her face became less and less revealing of her emotions, but Pat's and mine were a study in tragedy and loss.

On the night before she left, we were sitting in the den, quietly absorbed in our own thoughts. I don't know which of us started it, but soon we were both crying.

"It hurts so much to lose her."

"I know. I know. She's like our own daughter."

The next day came all too quickly, but we knew that we had to leave by noon in order to get to New York's JFK Airport on time for the plane, so we worked diligently to see that all of Tran's bags were packed properly. She insisted on wearing clothes which were similar to those she had worn on the day she arrived. Those clothes had long since been discarded as too small, so we found others in a shop in an Asian section of Arlington. Her face began to betray some emotion as she thrust out her chin defiantly, trying to hide her fears. Then her face became serious, her lower lip pulled slightly in.

"I've been happy here," she said.

We were interrupted by the postal letter carrier, who handed our one piece of mail to Pat. She opened it with a wary look on her face. I noticed that the envelope and handwriting were similar to those of the original letter from Tran's distant relative.

"It doesn't change things," Pat said as she finished the letter. "He says that we won't have to worry about Tran's safety. His mother is being sent to Canada. Well, there won't be any bombs. That's something to be grateful for. Tran is supposed to join his mother in Canada. I guess we'll have to change plans."

Tran, however, was suddenly animated. "Then I don't have to go!"

"You don't? But you said you had to. Don't you want to go now?"

"She was a very old lady, and I thought that she would be alone in the bombings. I thought I would be able to protect her. But now that she's going to be in Canada . . ."

"I never knew that was how you felt," I said in amazement.

She seemed a little embarrassed. "I was afraid. I mean, I thought I could protect her, and I thought my duty was to be with her in a time of trouble. She is part of my family. All these things, but I was afraid, too, and I didn't want to show my fear. Oh, I don't know what I mean, but I know that my decision to stay here is a correct one. Will you let me stay? I want to be a part of this family."

"You're quite a person, Tran," Pat said proudly, beaming through her tears, "and you'll always have a place here in this family. You've made a very good decision."

Comprehension

1. Who was Tran? With whom did she live? Where?
2. How had Tran come to live in the United States? Why?
3. What happened to Tran's parents? How did she react to the news?
4. How did Tran adjust to life in the United States?
5. What did the letter from Tran's relative say?

45

6. What did Tran decide after reading the letter? What reason did she give for this decision?
7. How did each member of the family behave during the week before Tran's intended departure?
8. Describe the scene just prior to the departure for JFK.
9. What caused Tran to change her mind? What had her true reason for wanting to go away been?
10. What was Tran's final decision? How was it received by Pat and Andy?

Exercises

A. Use each of the following terms in a sentence:
long since, to become accustomed to, to be well acquainted with, guerilla raid, malnutrition, to supersede, statewide, spelling bee, to be fond of, war-torn, surely, duty, decision, mispronunciation, to slice, upside down, nonstop, to thrust out, quite a person.

B. A common ending which is used to change adjectives to nouns is *-ness.*

He's always very *kind;* he shows his *kindness* in many ways.

Change the following adjectives to nouns by adding *-ness.* Then use each word in a sentence.

Example: seriousness   She always has a look of *seriousness* on her face.

1. serious	6. polite
2. foolish	7. eager
3. happy	8. late
4. sad	9. quick
5. sharp	10. close

C. Match the term in the left column with its OPPOSITE in the right column.

Example: c 7. south   c. north

___ 1. ashamed	a. late
___ 2. small	b. sadness
___ 3. similar	c. north
___ 4. happiness	d. cowardly

___	5. brave	e. infrequently
___	6. afraid	f. short
___	7. south	g. large
___	8. often	h. different
___	9. early	i. proud
___	10. long	j. fearless

Discussion

1. Name some countries in Southeast Asia. What languages are spoken there?
2. What is a refugee? Why are there refugees? Where do they go? What are the purposes of refugee camps?
3. What are some difficulties of becoming a citizen of another country? Of adapting to another culture? Of becoming a member of another family?
4. Do you think that Tran's original decision was right? Why?
5. What do you think life is like in Southeast Asia today? In Canada? How do you think life in these areas compares to life in your country? In the United States?

Unit 9: Ten Steps

Robert Little

I put on a clean pullover, a light blue one with a small alligator on the pocket. I got it from the third drawer in the antique chifforobe which we found while on vacation in Maine last summer. I was in our bedroom on the second floor of our suburban house. I could look out the window and see the Cresseys' yard and their dog, Christopher Robin, a large black, friendly mutt. Only the dog wasn't there. I lingered a moment and then went into the small bathroom off the bedroom to wash my face.

The soap was liquid. It came out of a plastic bottle that was called "Soap in a Bottle" or something like that. It was a new product for us; we'd never tried it before. Gina loved to try new gimmicks. I dried my hands and put the hand towel on the left-hand side of the towel rack. I always put it there. A creature of habit, I suppose. The rack looks loose; someday it will fall down and break. The faucet drips because I never got around to replacing a worn washer. I shut the door when I left the bathroom so I wouldn't have to hear the drip-drip-drip.

I went back into our bedroom and looked around the room, taking it all in. On the bed was Gina's stuffed Snoopy dog. She's had that dog for so long now that I forget when and where she got it. I reached down to touch its floppy ears and it fell onto the floor. When I stooped over to pick it up, I noticed a black mark on the wall behind the bed. The bed hits the wall every time someone gets into it, and it makes marks on the wall. I put the dog back onto the bed, but it fell off again as I left the room.

For a moment I couldn't remember the color of the wallpaper in the hallway, so I shut my eyes and tried to remember, tried to picture it. I couldn't. I opened my eyes and saw that, of course, it was that dull green and blue striped design that we had put up when James was still in high school.

I went into James's now-empty room and looked around. We had cleaned out the room completely, so that the only thing I could see was a fly on the windowsill. I opened the window and shooed it out. I then measured the room by walking across from one wall to the other in each direction. It is ten by fourteen.

I went into the family room, with its deep-pile shag rug, and crossed to the desk. Another old-timey piece of furniture. It has a roll-top with dozens of little cubicles and small drawers. Right out in the open, so no one could miss it, I placed a large manila envelope which I had prepared for Gina. I had put instructions, money, deeds, etc., inside. On the outside, I marked "For Gina."

The curtains in this room were red. Where the sun hits them they are now pink, not red. There was a magazine on the coffee table, a recent issue of *Newsweek*. There was also a copy of this week's *TV Guide* on top of the color television. We usually kept it on top of the box which controls our cable TV hookup, but I left it where it was.

The room was functional and comfortable. At one end there were two easy chairs that faced each other. I sat in one, but rose quickly and left the room, heading for the kitchen.

Gina was there looking up a recipe for peach cobbler. She promised Sarah, our neighbor, that she'd make her special cobbler for Sarah's party tomorrow night. She was also defrosting a roast in the microwave for tonight's dinner. I used to like to cook, too, but lately, I've gotten away from it. Gina didn't look up when I entered. She didn't look up as I crossed to leave by the back door either, but she said, "If you're going to the Giant, will you pick up some whole wheat flour?" I mumbled my assent and went out to the garage. It wasn't connected to the house but was about fifteen yards behind it.

As I walked to the garage, I saw the Risher kid playing with some toys in the sandbox in their backyard. He was running the toy truck back and forth through the sand. The sand was wet and it covered both him and his toys. I watched him, noted his intensity for a few minutes, and then said, "So long, Michael," but he didn't answer. He was too busy with the sand and the truck.

Then I went to the garage and unlocked the door. I walked around our VW Rabbit, running a soft cloth over it, polishing it and cleaning the windows. It had been a faithful car over the years. Not too much power, but steady and reliable. I noticed a few scratches on the door. Then I looked around the rest of the garage at the junk we had accumulated. I made a mental inventory of all the tools, boxes, playthings, patio furniture, and car accessories that seemed to cover every available space in the building. I stood there a few moments longer and then closed the doors and walked up to the front of the house and looked at my watch. It was 9:45.

The front yard had seen a lot of use in its day. At one time, we even had a small vegetable garden there. I think I liked that part of our home the best. It was part of our home, yet it looked out onto Stanford Street and allowed for the rest of the world to pass by. Or to drop over to visit, as many often did.

Around the side of the house we had built some stairs which led down to the side street below. I walked down these steps and counted. Ten. Ten steps. I thought I had counted correctly but wasn't sure. I'd better do it again. Never mind. I walked down the street and looked back at the house. One of the upstairs windows had a shade which was halfway down. I wanted to go back and count the steps again to make sure I had done it correctly, but I didn't.

I walked down to Wisconsin Avenue and then over to Bradley Boulevard and got on the bus. I got off at Montgomery Avenue

and walked up to the police station. I asked for Captain Maldonado and told him that if he was still looking for the man who
had killed Roger Maguire, then he should arrest me, since I had
done it.

Captain Maldonado questioned me for over an hour and then
finally said that I should write out a full confession and that if I
wanted the assistance of a stenographer, I could have it. He also
said that I could make such a confession on a videotape if I so
chose. I chose to write it out by myself.

Before I write it all down, about how I killed Maguire and
when and where and why, I want to write down the last things
I remember about my house and my wife and my neighbors. I'll
want to remember them because I won't ever see them again.
It's important to me.

Comprehension

1. Where are the ten steps that are referred to in the title of
   the story?
2. What crime has the narrator committed?
3. Why did he carefully observe all the minor details of his
   house?
4. What details can you remember about his bathroom? Bedroom? Hallway?
5. Who was James? What was in his room? How large is the
   room?
6. What did the narrator notice in the family room?
7. What was the narrator's wife doing when he went into the
   kitchen? What did she say to him?
8. Whom did he see in his neighbor's backyard? What was the
   child doing?
9. What did he do when he went into the garage?
10. How did he feel about the front yard of his house?

Exercises

A. Use each of the following terms in a sentence:
   pullover, antique, mutt, gimmick, towel rack, creature of
   habit, to picture something, windowsill, to shoo something
   out, shag rug, roll-top desk, out in the open, cable TV
   hookup, microwave, so long, reliable, patio furniture, to
   drop over, confession.

51

B. A common prefix which is used to change a noun or an adjective into a verb is -en (-em before b, m, or p), meaning *make*.

> They want to be *sure* that they are correct.
> They want to *ensure* their correctness.

Change the following nouns or adjectives to verbs by adding -en or -em. Then use each word in a sentence.

Example: enrich   Reading can *enrich* your knowledge.

1. rich
2. able
3. bitter
4. large
5. feeble

6. rage
7. slave
8. power
9. dear
10. act

C. Circle the word in parentheses which best completes the sentence.

Example: A pullover is a (joke/ (sweater) /hat/pair of socks).

1. A mutt is a (dog/cat/fish/bird).
2. Plastic is a (living/organic/synthetic/breathing) material.
3. We use towels to (eat with/dry ourselves/play with/cover pillows).
4. A faucet is usually found in a (drawer/bedroom/TV/sink).
5. A room which is 10 by 14 is (24/48/140/280) square feet in area.
6. Directions for preparing a certain type of food or meal are called a (recipe/cobbler/flour/roast).
7. A microwave oven is most likely to be found in a (family room/kitchen/patio/bedroom).
8. The most appropriate place to use patio furniture is (in the living room/in the garage/outside/in a vegetable garden).
9. A fly is a kind of (bird/plane/cloud/insect).
10. Another name for a family room is a (den/living room/bedroom/garage).

Discussion

1. Why did the narrator leave the envelope for his wife? What items, in addition to those mentioned, do you think were inside?
2. What is a family room? What are some of its uses?
3. Describe the various rooms and hallways in your house.
4. Which room in your house do you spend the most time in? Which room does your family congregate in the most? Which is your favorite room?
5. In most of this story, there is nothing but a simple, past-tense description of a man's journey through his home—not much of a plot. When did you first suspect that there was something unusual going on? What made you suspicious?

Unit 10: The Wrong House

James N. Young

The night was dark. And the house was dark. Dark—and silent.
The two men ran toward it quietly. They slipped quickly through
the dark bushes which surrounded the house. They reached the
porch, ran up the steps, and knelt down, breathing heavily, in
the dark shadows. They waited, listening.

Silence. Perfect silence. Then—out of the blackness—a
whisper: "We can't stay out here. . . . Take this suitcase. . . .
Let me try those keys. We've got to get in!"

Ten . . . twenty . . . thirty seconds. With one of the keys,
the first man opened the door. Silently, the two men entered
the house, closed the door behind them, and locked it.

Whispering, they discussed the situation. They wondered if they had awakened anyone in the house.

"Let's have a look at this place. Careful, Hy. I hope there isn't anybody awake!" And the soft rays of a flashlight swept the room.

It was a large room. A living room. Rugs, carefully rolled, lay piled on one side. The furniture—chairs, tables, couches—was covered by sheets. Dust lay like a light snow over everything.

The man who held the flashlight spoke first. "Well, Blackie," he said, "we're in luck. Looks as if the family's away."

"Yeah, gone for the summer, I guess. We better make sure, though."

Together they searched the house. They went on tiptoe through every room. There could be no doubt about it. The family *was* away. Had been away for weeks.

Yes, Hy Hogan and Blackie Burns were in luck. Only once in the past ten days had their luck failed them. It had been with them when they made their big robbery—their truly magnificent robbery—on the Coast. It had been with them during their thousand-mile trip eastward, by car.

It had been with them every moment—but one.

That moment had come just one hour before. It came when Blackie, driving the car, ran over a policeman. And Blackie, thinking of the suitcase at Hy's feet, had driven away. Swiftly.

There had been a chase, of course. A wild, crazy chase. And when a bullet had punctured the gasoline tank, they had had to abandon the car. But luck or no luck, here they were. Alone, and without a car, in a completely strange town. But safe and sound—with the *suitcase.*

The suitcase lay in the center of the table, in the center of the room. In it, neat little package on neat little package, lay nearly three hundred thousand dollars.

"Listen," said Hogan. "We have to get a car. Quick, too. And we can't steal one: It's too dangerous. We have to buy one. That means that we have to wait until the lots open. That will be about eight o'clock in this town."

"But what are we going to do with that?" Burns pointed to the suitcase.

"Hide it right here. Sure! Why not? It's much safer here than with us—until we get a car."

And so they hid the suitcase. They carried it down to the basement and buried it in an unfinished corner where no cement had been laid. Just before dawn, they slipped out.

As they were walking down the street, Hogan remarked that a Samuel W. Rogers lived in the house they had just left.

"How do you know?"

"Saw the name on some of them library books. The guy's really got a lot of books. Looks like a library in there."

The used car lots opened at eight, as they had supposed. Shortly before nine, Hogan and Burns had a car. A nice little car. Very quiet. Very inconspicuous. Very speedy. They arranged for temporary plates and drove off.

Three blocks from the house, they stopped. Hogan got out. Walked toward the house. He'd just go around to the rear, he thought, and slip in.

Fifty yards from the house, he stopped. Stared, swore softly. The front door was open. The window shades were up. The family had returned!

Well, what bad luck! And what could they do? Break into the cellar that night, and pick up the suitcase? No—too dangerous. Hogan would have to think of something.

"Leave it to me, kid," he told Burns. "You drive the car. I'll do the special brain work. Let's find a telephone. Quick!"

Ten minutes later, Hogan was consulting a telephone directory. Yes, there it was—Samuel W. Rogers, 555-6329.

A moment later he was talking to the surprised Mr. Rogers.

"Hello," he began, "is this Mr. Rogers—Mr. Samuel Rogers?"

"Yes, this is Mr. Rogers."

Hogan cleared his throat. "Mr. Rogers," he said—and his tone was sharp, official, impressive—"this is Headquarters, Police Headquarters, talking. I am Simpson. Sergeant Simpson, of the detective division . . ."

"Yes, yes!" came over the wire.

"The Chief—the Chief of Police, you know," here Hogan lowered his voice a little—"has ordered me to get in touch with you. He's sending me out with one of our men to see you."

"Am I in trouble of some kind?" asked Mr. Rogers.

"No, no, no. Nothing like that. But I have something of great importance to talk to you about."

"Very well," came the voice of Mr. Rogers. "I'll wait for you."

"And, Mr. Rogers," Hogan cautioned, "please keep quiet about this. Don't say anything to anybody. You'll understand why when I see you."

On the way back to the house, Hogan explained his idea to Burns.

Within ten minutes, "Sergeant Simpson" and "Detective Johnson" were conversing with the surprised Mr. Rogers. Mr. Rogers was a small man. Rather insignificant. He had pale blue eyes. Not much of a chin. A funny little face. He was nervous —a badly frightened man.

Hogan told the whole story. Somewhat changed, of course. Mr. Rogers was surprised, but he was delighted to be able to help the police.

He accompanied Hy Hogan to the cellar. And together they dug up the suitcase. Took it to the living room, opened it, saw that it had not been touched—that it really did hold a small fortune. Bills, bills, bills!

Hogan closed the suitcase.

"And now, Mr. Rogers," he announced, in his best official manner, "Johnson and I must run along. The Chief wants a report—quick. We have to catch the rest of the robbers. I'll keep in touch with you."

He picked up the suitcase and rose. Burns also rose. Mr. Rogers also rose. The trio walked to the door. Mr. Rogers opened it. "Come on in, boys," he said pleasantly—and in walked three men. Large men. Strong men. Men in police uniforms who, without fear, stared at Hy Hogan and Blackie Burns.

"What does this mean, Mr. Rogers?" asked Hogan.

"It's quite simple," said Mr. Rogers. "It just happens that *I* am the Chief of Police!"

Comprehension

1. In the first few paragraphs of the story, how do we know that the two men are breaking into the house?
2. What did they conclude about the residents of the house? Why?
3. What caused them to abandon their car?
4. What was in the suitcase? Where and how did Hogan and Burns get it?

57

5. Where did they decide to hide the suitcase?
6. When did they buy a car? Where? What was it like?
7. What did they discover when they returned to the house?
8. Explain Hogan's plan to get the money back.
9. What did Hogan and Burns do when they got the suitcase back upstairs?
10. Why didn't their plan succeed?

Exercises

A. Use each of the following terms in a sentence:
to kneel down, to be in luck, to make sure, no doubt about it, to be away, to run over, safe and sound, dawn, to slip out, inconspicuous, to get in touch with, to be in trouble, to keep quiet, insignificant, trio, on the way back.

B. Some nouns ending in *-tion* or *-ment* may be changed to adjectives by adding *-al.*

> She went abroad for her *education.*
> She had some *educational* experiences while she was abroad.

Change the following nouns to adjectives by adding *-al.* Then use each word in a sentence.

Example: environmental   Air pollution is an *environmental* problem.

1. environment	6. tradition
2. government	7. ornament
3. vocation	8. occupation
4. division	9. conversation
5. recreation	10. addition

C. Match the term in the left column with the term which has a SIMILAR meaning in the right column.

Example: <u>a</u> 4. steps   a. stairs

___	1. robber	a. stairs
___	2. insignificant	b. fast
___	3. abandon	c. make a hole
___	4. steps	d. desert
___	5. terrified	e. middle
___	6. puncture	f. speak softly

58

   __ 7. silly   **g.** thief
   __ 8. center   **h.** unimportant
   __ 9. speedy   **i.** foolish
  __ 10. whisper   **j.** frightened

Discussion

1. Many of the sentences in this story aren't true sentences; for example, in the second paragraph: "Silence. Perfect silence." What quality does this writing technique add to the story?
2. What can you tell about the character and education level of Hogan and Burns from their dialogue?
3. What else might the robbers have done to retrieve the suitcase? What would you have done?
4. What would you have done if you had been Chief of Police Rogers?
5. What precautions do you or your family take at home when you go away on vacation?

Unit 11: Irene's Sister

Vina Delmar

It had been fifteen years since I'd seen my friends on Rigel Space Colony IV. I looked forward to my return. This is a story of those days, fifteen years ago.

It was the year 2089, the year the schools didn't open on time, the year the plague of space fever descended and caught us. We were as defenseless as if we were inhabitants of some medieval city faced with a new and terrible sickness.

I was only a young girl at the time. My friends and I were confused and frightened, but our parents had no answers. They were as terrified as we. "All we know is that it's some kind of space fever," they told us. "It either kills you or leaves you crippled forever. Don't get too close to anyone or anything strange. You can't be too careful."

Fear held us so completely that we forgot how to laugh or

play. I can remember lying in bed at night waiting for the disease to strike me. I had no idea what form it might take and I lay very quietly, praying that when I next wished to move my legs or arms, I would be able to do so as I had always done in the past.

There was one among us, however, who had no fear of the terrible plague. That girl was Irene Crane. In my mind's eye, I can still see her as she was back there in those difficult days. She was a yellow-haired child with a happy ring to her laughter and the greatest capacity for fun of anyone I've ever known. She was the school beauty, popular with teachers and students alike; and if she was not the most intelligent of our group, that was easily forgiven, for one does not expect to find genius in a flower.

Irene had a sister who was a year younger. Her mother called her Caroline, but outside the house she was known simply as Irene's sister. It was natural for her to be Irene's sister, just as it was natural for us to be a nameless group of girls known as Irene's friends. Irene was the center of our small world, and we revolved about her brilliance and asked for no recognition for ourselves. Irene's sister, conscious of her inability to compete with the beauty and entrancing manner of Irene, was perfectly content to be only a pale reflection of our yellow-haired commander.

Only once were we at odds with Irene's way of thinking. That was when she said, "I'm not scared of that space fever. There's no way any of us will ever get it. You'll see. None of us will. We're invincible."

None of us agreed with her. We were a little ashamed of our fears of the terrible sickness which had befallen our small planet, but those fears were there just the same. They were with us day and night.

At least we had each other. Since we played together, went to school together, and knew each other since early childhood, there was nothing to fear by spending time together.

I can remember the day that we all went over to Ginny Smith's house for games and light refreshments. For our health's sake, the grown-ups looked upon the party with some doubts, but for the good of our morale they consented.

"After all," they said to one another, "it's the same group of girls who see each other almost every day anyway. It'll be all right."

"It's the same group except for Irene's sister." She hadn't been invited because she was not in our grade at school, and Ginny Smith hadn't known that Irene had a sister.

"It doesn't matter," Irene said. "Caroline isn't feeling well. She has an upset stomach, I guess."

The games were fun. We played three-dimensional electronic chess, and there was a hilarious round of hide-behind-the-time-warp which left all of us laughing. The food was great, too. Ginny's parents are really wonderful cooks. We also danced. Of course, Irene was the group's best dancer. She taught us a new rock dance which she had learned on her recent trip back to Earth with her grandparents. We listened to that wonderful singing group, Cherie and the Asteroids.

It was a beautiful day. We all seemed to forget for a while that something strange and terrible walked everywhere on our small colony deep in space. We forgot for a few hours the dangers that lay beyond Ginny's dome house. We were just getting ready to leave and thanking Ginny for a lovely party when the video-phone beeped.

I can still see Ginny's mother as she stood talking to Irene's mother on that phone. There was a look of horror on both women's faces. I can still see the tears in their eyes. We couldn't hear what they were saying, probably because we wanted to avoid and ignore what was obviously bad news.

"Irene," she said in a choked voice, "that was your mother. Your sister has caught the space fever. You can't go home; it's too dangerous. You'll have to stay here." There was a horrible pause. Then, "It's too late for us to be afraid of you, child. You've been here all day."

We went away without touching Irene, some of us without speaking to her. The plague had reached out and struck at us. We hurried home afraid of each other, ashamed of our fear, and unable to keep back the thought that tomorrow we would all be attacked by death or lameness.

Irene stayed with the Smiths, I suppose. I don't know. I hurried home and wrote an emotional, crazy little letter. My father had recently been transferred to a more distant space colony. He was an engineer with the United Earth Command. He specialized in gravity problems and in solving them. He and my mother had gone off to the new planet and left me with an aunt and uncle so that I could finish school on Rigel. Now I no longer wanted to stay. My letter begged my father to come and get me and take me to safety somewhere, anywhere. I did not know that the plague was widespread. I thought it was only on our colony. Anyway, both my parents came and took me away. I went happily and thankfully, not knowing that it would be fifteen years before I set foot on Rigel again.

On my first night back, which was last night, I stayed with an old friend, Maureen Morales. I was surprised to find that Maureen's living room was set up for a party.

"Just the old group," she explained, "and their husbands and boyfriends. You remember Ginny Smith; she'll be here. So will Lila Day, Sally Mullen, the Crane sisters, and the rest of the old group."

A strange feeling of terror ran through me at the mention of the Crane girls. I was a child again, frightened before a terrible, mysterious force that wanted to kill me.

"I remember them all," I said. "How are the Crane girls?"

"The same as ever, just exactly the same. One popular and one a complete failure."

"That's not fair," I protested. "Caroline had the space fever. I'm surprised that she's even alive. How can you expect her to . . ."

"But it's Irene who's the failure. She's even a little ridiculous for a grown woman. Remember how she used to laugh and play jokes and be the life of any party? Well, she's still the same, only the jokes are old and stale, and everything she says comes out sounding silly. But we have discovered that you can't invite Caroline without inviting Irene, so . . ."

"But, you mean that Caroline is well?"

"Of course she is. She had good care and good sense used on her, and she's as fine as anyone. A lot finer, I guess. She went through so much pain and suffering that she has more depth and understanding than most people. She's so strong and dependable. Of course, she thanks her doctor and her nurse and her mother for everything, and they say that it was Caroline's patience and courage that helped them to help her. Wait till you see her. She's—"

It was at that moment that the front door scanner told us that someone was approaching. Maureen's husband saw it first, but he was busy preparing a punch for the party, so he called out, "Maureen, would you get the door, please? It's Caroline's sister."

Comprehension

1. Where does this story take place? When?
2. What is the "plague" that the author refers to in this story?
3. Why was Irene Crane so popular as a child?
4. How did Caroline feel about her sister?
5. What did the girls do at the party at Ginny Smith's house?
6. Why wasn't Caroline at the party?
7. What did Mrs. Crane call Mrs. Smith about?
8. Why did the narrator write to her father? What was the result?
9. What had Maureen arranged for the narrator's return to Rigel? Who was going to be there?
10. What is the significance of the last sentence in the story?

Exercises

A. Use each of the following terms in a sentence:
to look forward to, on time, medieval, to be at odds with, genius, to be ashamed of, for the good of, grown-up, after all, upset stomach, three-dimensional, colony, dome, gravity, widespread, to set foot on, to be set up for, the life of the party.

B. Many English words can be used as either a verb or a noun without any change in form.

> We're going to *record* our voices on that tape.
> Did you play the *record* of that new rock group?

Use each of the following words first as a verb and then as a noun.

1. work		6. lock
2. help		7. light
3. experiment		8. hurry
4. play		9. dream
5. watch		10. knock

C. Fill in the blanks with a word from the list.

> *Example:* All of my parents' children are girls; I don't have any *brothers*.

aunt	grandfather	nephew
brother	grandmother	sister
brother-in-law	great-uncle	sister-in-law
cousin	niece	uncle

1. My sister's daughter is my _____.
2. My father's mother is my _____.
3. Your mother's brother is your _____.
4. Your grandfather's brother is your _____.
5. If your mother's sister had a child, that child would be your _____.
6. My father's sister is my _____.
7. I hope our baby is a girl; then our son will have a _____.
8. When I got married, my husband's sister became my _____.
9. My brother's son is my _____.
10. Your mother's father is your _____.

Discussion

1. Do you think people will be living on other planets or in space colonies in the next century? Why?
2. What diseases are as dangerous and as frightening as the one in the story?
3. Why is it that adversity, such as a severe illness, seems to make some people stronger?
4. Do you know any brothers or sisters who are like Irene and Caroline (when they were young)? What is their relationship like?
5. The story mentioned some household products (videophone, front door scanner, etc.) which might be used in the future. What other developments do you envision for our future?

Unit 12: Detour to Romance

Gilbert Wright

The Air and Space Museum, which is part of the Smithsonian Institution in Washington, D.C., is the most visited museum in the United States. Year after year, more people visit this massive exhibit honoring the men and women who have pioneered flight and the exploration of space than visit any other monument or museum in the entire country.

I work in a little room off the main entrance to the museum, checking coats and other articles which people do not want to carry around as they tour the building. I see virtually everyone who enters the museum.

Maryanne Wilson, who used to sell souvenirs at the stand

located next to my checkroom, has studied the laws of probability because she likes to bet. She claims that she can calculate, according to her system, the odds against anything happening. She calculated once that if I held my job for 112 more years, I would know everyone in the United States by sight.

I myself came to the conclusion that at the very least, if I waited long enough, I would see everyone who traveled. I've told people this theory for years, but no one ever did anything about it. No one except Sidney, that is. Sidney came into the museum a little over three years ago.

There are several short films which are shown at the museum every half hour. The one called *To Fly* is the most popular, and people line up hours in advance to see a particular showing. Sidney was waiting at the head of the line for the 1:05 showing one afternoon. He was standing there looking very nervous.

I remember noticing him that first day. He wasn't much more than a thin, anxious kid, but there was something about him. It was eerie. I knew. I just knew that he was meeting his girlfriend and that they were going to go off and be married that same day. There's no use in my trying to explain how I knew this, but after one has watched people for eighteen years, as I have, it's easy.

Well, more tourists poured through the front door, so I got busy. I didn't look up again until it was nearly time for the 1:35 showing of *To Fly*. I was surprised to see that the young fellow was still there, at the head of the line.

Sidney's girlfriend wasn't there for the 2:05 either, nor the 2:35, and when the viewers of the 3:05 showing were leaving the theater, Sidney was looking pretty desperate. Soon he wandered over near my window, so I called out and asked him if I could help.

He described her in a loving way. "She's small and dark, nineteen years old, and has a spirited face. I mean she can get mad, but she never stays mad for long. She has a short coat made of soft brown leather, but maybe she's not wearing it."

I couldn't remember seeing anyone like her.

He showed me a letter, actually a postcard, from her: "I'll be there Thursday. Meet me at the museum. Let's fly. Love, love, love, love, Kate." It was from Omaha, Nebraska.

"Why don't you phone home? She's probably called there, since she missed you here."

67

He looked ill. "I've only been in town two days. We were going to meet and then drive to Florida, where I've got a job promised me. I have no address." He touched the postcard. "I got this general delivery." And with that, he walked back to the head of the line to look over the people going to the 4:35 show.

When I came on duty the next day, he was still there.

"Did she work anywhere?" I asked.

He nodded. "She was a gardener. I called her former boss, but all he knows is that she left to get married."

Well, that's how it began. Sidney hung around that line and the museum for the next three or four days. The D.C. police looked into the case, but they couldn't do much; after all, no crime had been committed. Maybe she had just changed her mind, they reasoned. Somehow I didn't believe that.

One day, after about two weeks, I told Sidney of my theory. "If she's a traveler, and if you wait long enough, you'll see her coming through that door someday." He turned and looked at the front entrance as though he had never seen it before, while I went on explaining about Maryanne's figures on the laws of probability.

Sidney went to work for Maryanne as a clerk. "I had to get a job somewhere, didn't I?" he said sheepishly. Neither of us ever spoke of Kate anymore, and we dropped the subject of the laws of probability, but I noticed that Sidney observed every person who entered that most visited of all museums.

Maryanne tired of life in the nation's capital about a year later, and she moved to New Mexico. Sidney took over the stand, expanded it, and soon had a very nice little business.

Then came yesterday. It was spring and the tourists had descended on Washington, as they do every year. There was an endless stream of them, as usual. What made yesterday different began with a great noise.

Sidney cried out and the next thing I knew, there were souvenirs and cards, dolls, and who-knows-what flying all over the place. Sidney had leaped over the counter and upset everything in sight. He ran across the floor and grabbed a young woman who was standing not ten feet from my window. She was small and dark and had an interesting face.

For a while they just hung on to each other, laughing and

crying and saying things which had no meaning. She'd say a few words like, "It was the other one, the one down the street, the one called the castle on the mall," and he'd kiss her speechless and tell her the many things he'd done to try to find her. What apparently had happened, three years ago, was that Kate had gone to a different building. When she was young, her family had taken her to a part of the Smithsonian where the plane in which Charles Lindbergh had flown across the Atlantic Ocean was. She remembered where it was, but she didn't think that they would move it. She had waited at another museum for days and had spent all her money trying to find Sidney. Finally, she got a job as a gardener with the Department of the Interior, working on the grounds of various government buildings around town.

"You mean you've been here all the time?" Sidney gasped incredulously.

She nodded.

"But everybody visits the Air and Space Museum! You mean you've been here for three years and never come through those doors before? I've been here all the time, waiting and waiting for the day to come, watching everyone who came here. . . ."

She began to look pale. She looked over at the doors and said in a weak voice, "No, I've never been in here before. But Sidney, for almost three years I've been working on the grounds around this very building! I've thought about coming in here often, but I never did before today. I just never got around to it." Then she threw her arms around him and they both began to cry again.

What a wonderful drama had unfolded before my eyes! It's too bad Maryanne couldn't have seen it, too. The wonderful thing is how the laws of probability worked so hard and so long until they finally got Kate to walk through those front doors of ours.

Comprehension

1. Who was Maryanne? Why did she know about the laws of probability?
2. Why was Sidney at the Air and Space Museum?
3. Where is the museum? What is in it? Do many people visit it each year?

69

4. What is *To Fly?* How often is it shown? Why is there often a line?
5. Why were Sidney and Kate unable to get in touch with each other?
6. Were the police able to help Sidney? What did they reason? What did the narrator of the story believe?
7. Where did Sidney get a job? Why?
8. Where did Maryanne go? Why?
9. What happened when Sidney saw Kate for the first time in three years?
10. Why hadn't they met three years ago? What had Kate been doing for the past three years?

Exercises

A. Use each of the following terms in a sentence:
year after year, to pioneer, monument, to carry around, to know by sight, at the very least, every half hour, eerie, spirited, general delivery, to look over, to hang around, sheepishly, to drop the subject, endless stream, incredulously, grounds, to unfold.

B. Circle the term in parentheses which best completes the sentence.

Example: A small token of remembrance can be called a (movie/museum/ souvenir /castle).

1. If you grab something, you (install it/wait for it/go up to it/seize it roughly).
2. The best place to leave packages for a while is in (a garage/a magazine stand/a checkroom/an elevator).
3. A person who is mad is (small and dark/neat/excited/ angry).
4. We use (lamps/couches/sheets/dreams) on a bed.
5. Someone walking on tiptoe is probably trying to walk (well/quickly/carelessly/quietly).
6. Grown-ups are (children/youngsters/adults/parents).
7. An enchanting person is (healthy/scared/frightened/ charming).
8. If you whisper, you are (speaking softly/speaking loudly/ yelling/crying).

70

9. Someone who does something silently does it (impressively/well/quickly/noiselessly).
10. He wanted to borrow some money from me, but I didn't want to (ask/lend/need/beg) him any.

C. Adjectives of three or more syllables form their superlatives by the addition of *most*.

sentimental He is the *most sentimental* man I have ever met.

Use *most* to form the superlative of each of these adjectives. Then use the superlative form in a sentence.

1. beautiful
2. typical
3. natural
4. exciting
5. popular
6. professional
7. official
8. wonderful
9. successful
10. horrible

Discussion

1. Describe a time when you missed someone because you got your directions or instructions wrong. How did you find the person?
2. What are the laws of probability? How can they be helpful to people?
3. Would you enjoy visiting the Air and Space Museum? What other places of interest do you know about in Washington, D.C.?
4. What kinds of souvenirs do you buy when you visit an interesting place?
5. What does a gardener do? Do you enjoy gardening?

Unit 13: Final Break

Ian S. Thompson

Carson and Jane had been living together for eleven years. Alone. Just the two of them. He had been there whenever she needed him, taking care of her when she was sick, giving her emotional support, encouraging her in whatever she wanted to do.

Now she was going to leave.

They had been walking along Kingsford Street, not touching. Jane stopped and put her hand on his arm.

"This is the new bookstore I was telling you about. I thought you might find the sort of thing we spoke of here. I want to get something for you."

Carson nodded as though in a daze. There were tears in his eyes as he looked into the bookstore window. The purchase had been her idea, not his. He had wanted to explore this new discount store, but these circumstances were hardly conducive to browsing.

"What about this new Robert Ludlum thriller?" Jane pointed to a display near the front counter. "You've always enjoyed his work."

Carson trembled a little. One of the little things he loved so much about Jane was the truly genuine interest she had always taken in what he liked to read. It had made him feel young and somehow, loved, though in his heart he knew he was no longer young.

"Yes, yes, I have always enjoyed him, haven't I? He seems to come out with a new novel just frequently enough. I've always said that, haven't I?" He was feeling a bit self-conscious, and he avoided meeting her eyes because there was so much in his own that he didn't want her to see.

They continued looking up and down the aisles, bantering about the latest exposés by Hollywood stars, speculating on certain politicians' chances in upcoming elections as a result of their books, picking up whatever book caught their eyes.

By the time Jane began reading cartoons from the latest Garfield book, Carson was wishing that they had never come into the store in the first place. But Jane had been insistent. She wanted to give him something. A parting gift, she had called it.

She was smiling at him across a case of books, smiling out of green, clear, untroubled eyes. It surprised him. And yet, why should it, he asked himself as he aimlessly turned the pages of the new cookbook he was holding. He wasn't looking at anything on the pages. He had always tried to be modern, hadn't he, and modernity (or at least part of it) was to see these things through bravely, when and if they came.

These have been happy years, he thought. Oh, there were some ups and downs, but through it all, he'd been truly happy.

Five minutes later, they were out on the street again, out in the sunshine. After looking at her watch, Jane suggested an afternoon cocktail. There was an expression of excitement in her eyes which Carson couldn't quite place. "I know a place," she said, "You'll like it there."

It was a small, ordinary pub on one of the side streets. She ordered the house special for both of them.

She didn't speak, but she leaned across the table and took his hand. She smiled pleasantly and sincerely.

He didn't know what to make of it at first. Then he found himself striving to keep his wits about him.

They drank their cocktails quickly, then sat back as though relaxed, and looked off into space.

"You really should reconsider staying in the house alone. It's been too big for the two of us; surely you'll get lost rattling around there all by yourself. I feel bad about this. I wish there were something I could do to make it easier."

There was one thing he could have suggested, but his pride wouldn't let him. Besides, he didn't want her to have any feelings of regret, any pangs of conscience. It would taint all those wonderful years together.

"No," he said. "I'll be fine. Really. I'm the original Mr. Tough Guy, remember?"

But she didn't want to let the subject drop. She changed directions. "Another thing. I've been reluctant to mention this before now, but I want you to know that you'll never have to worry about money, if that ever becomes a problem. I know you're sensitive about that area, but I feel strongly about it, and I want you to know . . ."

"OK, OK. I understand what you're saying. And you're right. I am sensitive about money. I've always paid my own way. It's true, I have some difficulties now, but I don't expect you to do anything."

"Why not?" She brushed his arguments aside, "And John (she mentioned his name for the first time) agrees. We were talking about it last night."

John . . . we . . . How easily, how familiarly she said those words. And yet two months ago, they hadn't even met. Two months . . . was it really only two months since she'd gone on that job interview to Denver? A lot can change in a short time.

He'd realized after she'd returned that something had changed. It wasn't anything tangible, it was more of a feeling than anything else. They hadn't spoken of it, but he'd had a deep instinct that she was no longer his, that he was sharing her with someone else. Someone special to her.

He tried to imagine this John. Young, no doubt. Young, virile, and vibrant. Probably a good dancer or musician; she'd be attracted to qualities like those. And there was the appeal of the city, too. Life on the ranch was a good life, but he realized that it could also be dull for an attractive young woman. His thoughts drifted back to John. He hadn't met him yet, even though he had known of his existence for two months now.

John . . . He worked in the insurance business, she had told him. And smart, too; a clever, intelligent young man. Not that it mattered to Carson. Love was the key. If he loved her as deeply as Carson did—that was all that mattered. He was glad that the young man was smart and clever, but he was mostly concerned with her emotional needs.

Would he work to keep her happy? Would he be considerate of her, kind to her? Would he look at her with honest eyes like those of that young man over there? His attention was drawn to a handsome man who had just entered the restaurant. The fellow was looking around, hesitantly.

Then the young man stopped and looked directly at their table. Carson returned his gaze, his eyes widening in surprise as Jane rose to her feet. The lad was moving toward their table.

"So, you were able to get here after all, darling!" He heard Jane's voice greet him. They embraced briefly and then she turned to Carson. "Dad, this is John! This is the lucky bridegroom who's going to sweep your daughter off to the altar next week!"

Comprehension

1. What is the significance of the title of this story?
2. What was the relationship between Jane and Carson like?
3. What were they doing in the bookstore?
4. What kinds of books did they look at?
5. Where did they go after they left the bookstore? Why?
6. What was Jane's concern regarding Carson's living arrangements?
7. What had happened in Denver? How did Carson feel about it?
8. What did John do for a living? What kind of person was he?
9. What happened in the pub when John walked in?
10. Before the last paragraph, was there some doubt in your mind as to the relationships among the three characters? Why?

Exercises

A. Use each of the following terms in a sentence:
emotional, to walk along, in a daze, to be conducive to, in one's heart, self-conscious, exposé, upcoming, to catch one's eye, in the first place, when and if, house special, to keep one's wits about one, to let a subject drop, to pay one's own way, considerate.

B. The ending *-ive* can change some verbs into adjectives.

They *act* in a very busy manner. They're *active* people.

Change these verbs into adjectives by adding *-ive*. Then use each word in a sentence.

Example: impressive   His experience was *impressive* enough to get him the job.

1. impress	**6.** express
2. construct	**7.** correct
3. prevent	**8.** instruct
4. create	**9.** object
5. repress	**10.** attract

C. Direct discourse quotes the exact words spoken. Indirect discourse quotes words indirectly.

Direct: Jane said, "I know a good place."
Indirect: Jane said she knew a good place.

Change these sentences from direct to indirect discourse.

1. She said, "You'll like it there."
2. He said, "You've always enjoyed your work."
3. I said, "I want to get something for you."
4. I said, "You shouldn't get anything for me."
5. You said, "I want to meet John."
6. You said, "He agrees with me."
7. They asked us, "Do you want to buy these books?"
8. Jane said, "I don't want you to live here alone."
9. She said, "Don't you want to talk about this?"
10. We told her, "You're very sensitive about this."

Discussion

1. Do you think fathers are often upset when their daughters decide to marry? Why?

2. What would this story have been like if Carson were a mother and Jane were her son?
3. Where and how will (did) you introduce your fiancé (fiancée) to your parents?
4. Are you close to your opposite-sex parent? Will it be (Was it) difficult to leave that parent in order to get married?
5. What are *cocktails?* How many can you name?

Unit 14: A Case of Suspicion

Ed Wallace

He threw back the covers and sat up on his bed, his feet feeling along the cold floor for his house slippers, the telephone ringing insistently a little distance away.

He turned on the light and picked up the phone.

"This is Dr. Benson," he said.

The November wind was bringing sounds of winter as it blew around the little white house. The doctor got into his clothes, went to the table, and stared a moment at his watch, his spirit complaining at the job ahead of him.

2 A.M.

His mind complained at the hour and at why people in such remote, rural parts of the country chose such improper times to be born. He picked up his two satchels: the short pill bag, as the people of the town knew it, and the long obstetrical case—the baby bag, they called it.

He debated whether to bring his cigarettes. He knew he should stop, knew he was setting a bad example for people—a doctor smoking! Imagine! But old habits die hard. He put the pack in his pocket. The cold wind felt like a surgeon's knife at his face as he opened the door and ran, bending low, around the driveway to the garage.

His car started with difficulty, coughed a half-dozen times as he drove down the driveway, but then began to run more smoothly as he turned down Grass Street and onto the deserted highway.

Mrs. Ott Sorley, whom Dr. Benson was on his way to visit, already had almost a dozen children, but it seemed to the doctor that never once had she had a baby in good weather, nor in daylight. And while Dr. Benson was a country doctor, he was still a young man and couldn't find the pleasure that his father, "the old Doc Benson," had found in seeing Ott, the father, always two or three babies behind in the payment of his baby bills.

It was a long ride out to the Sorley farm and the sight of a man walking alone along the country road, as seen just ahead by the lights of the car, was a welcome relief to the doctor. He slowed down and looked at the man walking along with difficulty against the wind, a little package under his arm.

Coming alongside, Dr. Benson stopped and invited the man to ride. The man got in.

"Are you going far?" asked the doctor.

"I'm going all the way to Detroit," said the man, a rather thin man with small black eyes filled with tears from the wind. "Could you give me a cigarette?"

Dr. Benson unbuttoned his coat, then remembered the cigarettes in the outer pocket of his overcoat. He took out the package and gave it to the rider, who then looked in his own pockets for a match. When the cigarette was lighted, the man held the package a moment, then asked, "Do you mind, mister, if I take another cigarette for later?" The rider shook the package to remove another cigarette without waiting for the doctor to answer. Dr. Benson felt a hand touch his pocket.

"I'll put them back in your pocket," the little fellow said.

Dr. Benson put his hand down quickly to receive the cigarettes and was a little irritated to find them already in his pocket.

After a few minutes, Dr. Benson said, "So you're going to Detroit?"

"I'm going out to look for work in one of the automobile plants."

"Are you a mechanic?" asked the doctor.

"More or less. I've been driving a truck since the Vietnam War ended. But I lost my job about a month ago."

"Were you in the army during the war?"

"Yeah, I was a medic. Used to fly in medical helicopters right up into battle conditions. I saw a lot of action."

"Is that so?" said Dr. Benson. "I'm a doctor myself. Benson is my name."

"I thought this car smelled like pills," the man laughed. Then he added, more seriously, "My name is Corrigan."

They rode along silently for a few minutes, and the rider moved himself in his seat and placed his package on the floor. As the man leaned over, Dr. Benson caught his first good look at the small, catlike face.

The doctor also noticed the long, deep scar on the man's cheek, bright and red-looking as though it were of recent origin. He thought of Mrs. Ott Sorley and reached for his watch. His fingers went deep into his pocket before he realized that his watch was not there.

Dr. Benson moved his hand very slowly and carefully below the seat until he felt the leather holster in which he had an automatic handgun. Ever since he was robbed at gunpoint eighteen months ago, he always traveled with his gun under the seat. Especially late at night.

He drew the pistol out slowly and held it in the darkness at his side. When he had to slow down for a sharp bend in the road, he stepped on the brake hard and pushed the nose of the gun into his rider's side.

"Put that watch into my pocket," he said angrily.

The rider jumped with fear and put up his hands quickly. "My God, mister," he whispered. "I thought you . . ."

Dr. Benson pushed the pistol still deeper into the man's side and repeated coldly, "Put that watch in my pocket before I let this gun go off."

80

Corrigan reached for it, and with trembling hands, tried to put the watch into the doctor's pocket. With his free hand, Dr. Benson pushed the watch down into his pocket. He opened the door and forced the man out of the car.

"I'm out here tonight, probably to save a woman's life, but I took the time to try to help you," he said to the man angrily.

Dr. Benson started the car quickly and the wind closed the door with a loud noise. He put the pistol back into the leather holster under the seat and hurried on.

The drive up the mountain to the Sorley farm was less difficult than he had feared, and Ott Sorley had sent one of his older boys down the road with a lantern to help him across the old wooden bridge that led up to the little farmhouse.

Mrs. Sorley's many previous experiences with bringing children into the world apparently helped her greatly because she delivered this child with little difficulty, and there was no need on Dr. Benson's part for the instruments in the long bag.

When it was over, Dr. Benson gave in to his vice and sat down for a cigarette.

"A fellow I picked up hitchhiking on my way here tonight tried to rob me," he said to Ott. "He took my watch, but I somehow summoned my courage and pulled my gun on him. He quickly decided to give it back to me."

Ott smiled wide at such an exciting story coming from young Dr. Benson.

"Well, I'm glad he gave it back to you," Ott said. "Because if he hadn't, we wouldn't have any idea what time the child was born. What time would you say it happened, Doc?"

Dr. Benson took the watch from his pocket.

"The baby was delivered about thirty minutes ago, and right now it's . . ." He walked over to the lamp on the table.

He stared strangely at the watch in his hand. The crystal was cracked and the top was broken. He turned the watch over and held it closer to the lamp. He studied the worn inscription:

"To Corporal Tim Corrigan, Medevac Unit, whose personal bravery preserved our lives the night of Nov. 3, 1971, near Saigon on the Mekong River. Nurses Hohorst, Walsh, and Bryan."

Comprehension

1. At what time was Dr. Benson awakened by the phone? What time of year was it?
2. Who had called him? Why? How did he feel about it?
3. How did he feel about his smoking habit?
4. Why did Dr. Benson stop his car on the way to the Sorley farm?
5. What did the rider do with the doctor's pack of cigarettes?
6. What did the man do in the army?
7. How did the doctor get the watch from the man?
8. Was the delivery of the Sorley child difficult? Why?
9. Why did the doctor take the watch from his pocket?
10. Explain the irony of the story, particularly after the doctor read the inscription on the watch.

Exercises

A. Use each of the following terms in a sentence:
to sit up, to turn on, bad example, old habit, to slow down, to mind, more or less, helicopter, to see action, catlike, at gunpoint, automatic, bend in the road, to bring children into the world, to give in to, to summon one's courage.

B. A common ending among adverbs is *-ly*.

We always take *careful* notes in class.
We always take notes in class *carefully*.

Change the following adjectives to adverbs by adding *-ly*. Then use each word in a sentence.

Example: constant   The baby cries *constantly*.

1. constant
2. eager
3. slow
4. improper
5. silent
6. serious
7. profound
8. identical
9. fortunate
10. intimate

C. Circle the word in parentheses which best completes each sentence.

Example: A holster is a case used to hold (fruit/medicine/a watch/ (a gun)).

1. If a telephone rings insistently, it rings (off and on/ seldom/now and then/steadily).
2. A receiver is part of a (telephone/medicine bag/car/pistol).
3. My car needed to be repaired, so I took it to a (farmer/ druggist/mechanic/truck driver).
4. A (glasses/pill/watch/lantern) will help you see in the dark.
5. People who are debating an issue are (complaining/arguing over/driving/removing) it.
6. A doctor who specializes in obstetrics is concerned with (eyes/childbearing/broken bones/obesity).
7. When you lose something, you generally look (at it/for it/it up/it over).
8. Another word for *courage* is (silence/inscription/fear/ bravery).
9. A hitchhiker is a person hoping to get a free (ride/meal/ cigarette/watch).
10. If a place is remote, it is (near/beautiful/far/silent).

Discussion

1. Have you had any experiences with hitchhikers? Have you ever hitchhiked? What was it like?
2. How do you think the doctor felt after he read the inscription? What lesson could he have learned from this experience?
3. Are you generally suspicious of strangers? Would you like to be more (less) suspicious of people?
4. Are people in rural, remote places more or less trusting of people, in general, than people in big cities? Why?
5. Do you, or does someone in your family, own a gun? Why? What kind? Do you think people should be allowed to own handguns?

Unit 15: Better Late

Edward Stevenson

I had just completed work on my very first screenplay for a major Hollywood studio, and I was exhausted. Being a screenwriter was going to be harder than I thought. I reflected that I had had the hardest time writing dialogue for elderly people. After reading the travel section of *The New York Times* on my first Sunday back in the city, I decided to kill two birds with one stone. I would relax by taking an ocean cruise, and I would purposely sign onto a cruise where there were bound to be a lot of elderly folks. That way I could get some needed rest and also hone my dialogue-writing skills.

I was lucky. On our first day out, I met a fellow who must have been at least seventy-five. He was traveling with his wife, and he was a talker. As best as I can reproduce it, here's what he said to me as we met on the deck of the S.S. Helge, a Norwegian liner.

"Well, I'm certainly glad you're not seasick. When I first saw you leaning over the rail, I said to myself that you must be seasick, though I couldn't see how anybody could get seasick with the water so calm the way it is today. Our room steward says that anybody that gets seasick in this kind of weather wouldn't be safe on the lake in Central Park. He's a regular comedian. . . . And that reminds me, how much do you think I ought to tip him? The room steward, I mean. I'm not a person who has a lot of money, but still I want to do the right thing as to tipping.

"You see, this is the first time we've been on a boat—my wife and I, I mean. Of course, we've taken a trip up the Hudson with the kids, but I guess you wouldn't mention the Hudson River Day Line in the same breath with a big ship like this, would you? The kids thought it was wonderful, though. They're grown up and married now, with kids of their own—except Judy, that is, and she hardly has had time, not having been married a year yet —but it doesn't seem more than yesterday that they were running around and getting into all kinds of trouble. Time certainly flies . . .

"Whew! It's getting hot, isn't it? We must be coming into the tropics from the way it feels. Ever been down here before, Mr. —I don't think you mentioned your name, did you? Arthur? Well, I'm glad to know you, Mr. Arthur. My name's Bentham. I'd like you to meet my wife sometime, too. That's my wife sitting in that deck chair down at the end. She's making believe she's reading that book, but she's sound asleep. The salt air seems to make her very tired . . .

"As I was saying, time certainly flies. Now, you take me; why, it seems only the other day that Ellen and I were getting married; and here we are grandparents of six already.

"We've been married fifty years. It doesn't seem possible, but that's what it is, all right. Why, say, I can remember the wedding just as clearly as if it happened last week. It wasn't much of a wedding—you know, no ceremony and reception. Besides Ellen and me and the minister, there were only the minister's wife and the church janitor for witnesses. I can still see the five of us standing there in the chapel with the sun coming through the stained glass window, falling all around us, turning everything different colors. It was a long time ago, but the memory is still strong.

"Will you look at them flying fish! Aren't they the funniest things!

"When I look back, I think that Ellen and I must have been crazy, getting married the way we did. My goodness, I didn't have a cent to my name—it was all I could do to get together the money for the wedding ring. Engagement rings and honeymoons and all those special things were out of reach as far as we were concerned.

"I felt pretty bad, starting our marriage in a small efficiency apartment over a laundry. I wanted it to be better for us, and I told her so. A big wedding, a reception at the best hotel in New York, and a honeymoon in Miami or the Bahamas. She just laughed. 'If I wanted such riches, I'd have married a Rockefeller and not Johnny Bentham.' That's the way she was. And is. I didn't really mind not having a big church wedding, or a reception afterwards, but, gee, what's a wedding without a honeymoon? It made me feel low.

"But, you know, marrying that woman was the making of me. I was just a shipping clerk at the time; it was during the Great Depression, and I was lucky to have a job at all. Well, Ellen encouraged me to study accounting, and when an opening in the company came along, I stepped right into it. Today, folks call that 'upward mobility'; I called it 'being at the right place at the right time.'

"I retired as comptroller of that company last month. When I left the firm, they put on a dinner for me at the Plaza Hotel and gave me a watch. Here it is. See what it says, 'To John W. Bentham,' that's my full name, 'for fifty years of devoted service.' Mr. Stover, the president, made a speech. I did, too—but I was too choked up to say much. You can bet that I'd never have stayed in that company long enough to get that watch if it hadn't been for Ellen.

"And the kids, too, of course. When you get to be a family man you have to be a little more serious. Kit—that's short for Christopher—was the first; then Roger, Cynthia, Anthony, and Judy, the baby. Nice names, aren't they? Ellen picked them out.

"They're all grown up now—fine young men and women, if I do say so myself—but there were times when you just wondered if they ever would grow up. It was just one thing after another. Sick or healthy, they had you up to your neck in bills.

86

"Is that land over there to the left? No, I guess it's just clouds.

"Well, last year our company did pretty well and they gave all the old employees a month's pay for a bonus at Christmas—first bonus we had had in years. So what did I do? Well, I figured with all the kids married and no one to take care of but ourselves that we didn't have any real need for the money, so I didn't breathe a word about it to Ellen. You see, I'd been seeing those cruise advertisements in the papers and I thought to myself, that's just the thing for Ellen and me. Twelve days. Nassau and Jamaica for $750. I didn't say anything till about two weeks before we were about to sail. Then I broke the news. Well, you could have knocked Ellen over with a feather.

" 'Johnny Bentham,' she says, 'are you out of your mind?'

" 'No,' I says. 'And I haven't robbed a bank either.' So I told her all about the bonus.

"Well, she still thought I was crazy. 'Spending all that money on a little trip,' she says. 'Do you think we're millionaires? Johnny, I'll never set foot on that boat.'

" 'Now, that's a fine way to feel' I says, acting as if I were insulted. 'A woman refusing to go on a honeymoon with her husband!'

"Well, she just looked at me and I just looked at her, and first thing you knew she threw her arms around me and began kissing me, and what did the two of us do but end up laughing and crying like a couple of kids.

" 'Gee, Mama,' I says. 'It's better late than never, isn't it? . . .'

"Say, look at those flying fish!"

Mr. Bentham and I talked—actually, he talked and I listened —several more times during the cruise. I met Ellen, I met several other people their age, and I relaxed. Who could ask for more than that?

Comprehension

1. What does the narrator of the story do for a living? Why is he on the cruise?
2. How long have John and Ellen Bentham been married?
3. How did Bentham describe his wedding? What regrets did he have?

4. Where did the Benthams live right after they were married? How did Bentham feel about this?

5. What was Bentham's job when he got married? What did Ellen encourage him to do?

6. What did Bentham do last month? What position had he held prior to that?

7. How did his company reward him when he retired?

8. Where did the money for the Benthams' cruise come from?

9. How did John overcome Ellen's original objections to taking the cruise?

10. What is the significance of the title of the story?

Exercises

A. Use each of the following terms in a sentence:
screenplay, to kill two birds with one stone, cruise, to hone, to say to oneself, comedian, to grow up, to run around, to make believe, to be sound asleep, stained glass, honeymoon, efficiency apartment, upward mobility, devoted, bonus.

B. Circle the word in parentheses which best completes the sentence.

Example: The chief financial officer in a company is called the (clerk /(comptroller) /screenwriter/steward).

1. You usually give a (bonus/tip/message/watch) to a waiter or waitress.

2. If a body of water is calm, it is (smooth/choppy/rough/windy).

3. Someone who is choked up is about to (laugh/fall asleep/cry/sneeze).

4. A person who is exhausted is very (cold/hot/excited/tired).

5. To make believe is to (cancel/postpone/pretend/instruct).

6. *Sound asleep* means (sleeping lightly/half asleep/sleeping deeply/wide awake).

7. To mind something is to (like it/approve of it/insist on it/object to it).

8. A chapel is a small (ship/hotel/house/church).

9. The people who witness a marriage (avoid/observe/forget/calculate) it.

10. An eighty-year-old person is considered (middle-aged/retired/elderly/late).

C. Words like *down, over, out, under,* and *up* are often used as prefixes. Attach one or more of these prefixes to each of the following words. Then use each word in a sentence.

Example: paid   My boss told me I was *overpaid,* but I was actually *underpaid,* so I went out and found a job with a better salary.

1. put		6. fall
2. charge		7. hill
3. look		8. right
4. line		9. town
5. side		10. set

Discussion

1. Have you ever taken a cruise? Would you like to take one? Where would (did) you go?
2. What does a shipping clerk do? A comptroller?
3. What do you think of the concept of luck, or "being at the right place at the right time"? Are you a lucky person?
4. Do you know any people who have been married for fifty years? What are they like?
5. What is a depression? What do you know about the Great Depression which Bentham referred to? When was it? How did it affect your family?